Egypt's Parliamentary Elections, 2011-2012

A Critical Guide to a Changing Political Arena

Egypt's Parliamentary Elections, 2011-2012

A Critical Guide to a Changing Political Arena

EDITOR
Hesham Sallam

CONTRIBUTORS

Jadaliyya Egypt Page Editors
Ahram Online Egypt Elections Watch Editors
Jadaliyya Egypt Elections Watch Editors

Featuring a contribution by Wael Eskandar

TADWEEN PUBLISHING
Washington, DC

This publication is produced in part with the support of the Middle East Program at George Mason University, with which the Arab Studies Institute is affiliated. This publication also received support from the Center for Contemporary Arab Studies at Georgetown University.

Cover Image: A man walks past banners supporting candidates for the parliamentary elecitons in Cairo, Egypt on Monday, 28 November 2011. Voting began that day in Egypt's first parliamentary elections to take place since longtime authoritarian leader Hosni Mubarak had been ousted nine months earlier. (AP Photo/Bernat Armangue)

To the memory of Samer Soliman (1968-2012), a revolutionary scholar

CONTENTS

Acknowledgements

Egypt Elections Watch (EEW) was conceived through a joint vision that *Jadaliyya* and *Ahram Online* produced in order to provide readers with a critical perspective on Egypt's 2011/2012 parliamentary elections and the political context in which these elections were convened. I would like to thank the Center for Contemporary Arab Studies at Georgetown University and the Middle East Studies Program at George Mason University for believing in this vision and for generously supporting it by co-sponsoring the initiative.

Special thanks are due to members of EEW's editorial committee, Hani Shukrallah, Fouad Mansour, and Dina Samak of *Ahram Online*, and Mohamed Waked of *Jadaliyya*. These individuals have invested a great deal of time, energy, and leadership in building a unique vision for EEW, and bringing this vision to life. It was a great pleasure to serve on the editorial committee alongside this distinguished group.

Thanks are also due to the project's researchers—Gamal Essam El-Din, Mahienour ElMasry, Mary Mourad Shenouda, Osman El-Sharnoubi, Salma Shukrallah, Sherif Tarek, and Lilian Wagdy—who have worked tirelessly in preparing EEW's entries, and invested an enormous amount of research and thought in order to make the complexities of Egypt's political scene accessible to worldwide readership. This project would not have been possible if it were not for the commitment and brilliance of these talented writers. Special thanks are also due to Stephanie Gaspais for her much appreciated assistance in preparing the final results section.

EEW benefited from the support of a highly professional and dedicated group of copy-editors: Ian Doughlas, Adam Morrow, and Nabil Shawkat of *Ahram Online*, and *Jadaliyya*'s Lizette Baghdadi, Rosie Bsheer, Nabiha Das, Elizabeth Guthrie, and Sherene Seikaly. Each of these individuals has graciously worked on an unusually compressed schedule, sometimes spanning late nights, in order to bring clarity and precision to EEW's work.

I would also like to extend my thanks and gratitude to EEW's tech support team, Ahmed Mahmoud and the IT department of *Ahram Online*, including Ahmed Attress, Ahmed Farouk, and Hassan Hammad, *Jadaliyya*'s Ziad Abu-Rish, Bassam Haddad, Khalid Namez, Tom Sullivan, and Colleen Yeskovich, and members of Concepcion Design.

The biggest burden in managing this large operation fell on the shoulders of Project Coordinator Mary Mourad Shenouda, who worked closely with the editors, researchers, copy-editors, and tech support team in order to channel their respective efforts into what became the final product presented in this volume. There is not enough praise that could adequately recognize Mary's invaluable contribution to EEW.

Turning EEW's work into this edited volume involved a very onerous set of tasks, which Tom Sullivan kindly took on with great enthusiasm and professionalism.

This volume would have not been possible if it were not for Tom's diligence and commitment.

Special thanks are also due to Kaylan Geiger and Nehad Khader for their incredible support on the production process, and for proofreading this manuscript in full a number of times.

The final word goes to my fellow *Jadaliyya* co-editors and long-time friends Bassam Haddad and Ziad Abu-Rish, who have ushered this initiative toward success every step of the way. They have shown great patience and understanding in dealing with my—sometimes very demanding and tedious—requests, and for this they deserve all respect and recognition.

Hesham Sallam

Cairo, 5 August 2012

Introduction

Hesham Sallam

In a context in which emergency law, military trials of civilians, official bans on workers' strikes and demonstrations, chronic use of deadly violence against peaceful protesters by security forces, and frequent detention of political dissidents are all prevalent, it was hard to look at the 2011/2012 parliamentary elections in Egypt with anything but a healthy dose of skepticism. For many of those who were witnessing the lead-up to these elections, the vote signified a historic moment for Egyptians and a monumental step in the country's so-called transition to democracy. According to such perspectives, Egyptians were finally having a say in determining the future of their country in multiparty elections not managed by deposed president Hosni Mubarak or the now-defunct National Democratic Party (NDP).

For others, however, this event reflected the persistence of a political practice that Mubarak instituted long before his demise, namely the convening of elections with a view to impose a façade of democratic openness on a reality devoid of any democratic openness. This view becomes even more compelling once one considers that the elections ultimately failed to generate real checks on the authority of Egypt's military rulers, given that the powers of the parliament after the elections remained legally ambiguous and effectively limited. In June 2012 the Supreme Council of the Armed Forces (SCAF) dissolved parliament's lower house after a Supreme Constitutional Court ruling deemed the election of one-third of its seats unconstitutional. While longtime Muslim Brotherhood figure Mohamed Morsi was sworn in as president on 30 June 2012, his powers were constrained by the Constitutional Declaration of 17 June, which gave the military sweeping powers. President Morsi eventually repealed the declaration and retired some SCAF leaders on 12 August 2012, though it remains unclear the extent to which these moves will actually limit the non-democratic privileges of the military establishment in the long run. More importantly, whether or not successive elections and the emergent political arena will help Egyptians realize the goals of the January 25 Revolution, "bread, freedom, and social justice," is still an open question.

These opposing views are at the heart of an ongoing clash between two narratives on the state of Egypt's January 25 Revolution—a battle that any meaningful discussion of Egypt's 2011/2012 elections cannot overlook. One narrative, which (initially) the SCAF and (later) the Muslim Brotherhood have tried to promote through friendly media outlets, alleges that the January 25 Revolution has succeeded and that the time has come for protest movements to vacate public squares, the streets, and factories, and begin deferring to elite politics: elections, parliaments, and constitution writers. From this perspective, elections are viewed as an important step toward advancing the change that Egyptians have called for during the eighteen-day uprising that toppled Mubarak.

An opposing narrative, advanced by many dissident individuals and groups through demonstrations, strikes, and other forms of contentious political action posits that the revolution is far from complete and is under severe attack from the wielders of power. Advocates of this latter narrative tell us that the 2011/2012 elections are but a step toward normalizing and legitimizing a political reality in which Egypt's military rulers can steer the current "transition" in ways that secure their non-democratic privileges and those of other powerful, entrenched bureaucracies. Thus, proponents of this view feared that these elections would be used to abort rather than advance Egypt's inconclusive revolutionary struggle.

Even after Morsi took over as president, the tension between these two narratives has not subsided. By the end of December 2012, President Morsi signed into law a constitution that was drafted by an unrepresentative constituent assembly dominated by the Muslim Brotherhood and its allies at the exclusion of non-Islamist political communities that withdrew from the assembly in protest of the domineering role of Islamist groups in drafting the constitution. According to many observers, the constitution, which was approved in a constitutional referendum by about sixty-four percent of voters with a turnout rate that did not exceed thirty-three percent, placed limitations on individual rights and liberties, freedom of speech, and religious freedom, and rendered the military's budget and activities beyond the reach of conventional parliamentary oversight and accountability. The constitution was ratified in an environment in which Muslim Brotherhood leaders and allies were engaged in a campaign to slander their opposition, and stigmatize dissidents in ways that are not dissimilar to the tactics followed by the SCAF and, before it, the Mubarak regime. The constitution, moreover, fell short of delivering the promise of the January 25 Revolution for greater social and economic rights, especially at a time when Morsi and his sponsored government were preparing to conclude a controversial loan agreement with the International Monetary Fund (IMF). The agreement, which was negotiated behind closed doors with minimal transparency and little public deliberation, is reportedly poised to deepen the already widespread socio-economic grievances in Egyptian society by reinforcing the economic orientation and policies of the Mubarak regime. In sum, the battle between the narrative of a "continuing revolution" and the narrative of a "revolution accomplished" persists until this day, and the quest for "bread, freedom, and social justice" continues.

Taking the contested meaning and significance of the 2011/2012 parliamentary elections as a point of departure, *Jadaliyya*'s Egypt Elections Watch (EEW) project, launched in partnership with *Ahram Online*, and co-sponsored by the Center for Contemporary Arab Studies at Georgetown University and the Middle East Studies Program at George Mason University, offers a critical perspective on Egypt's 2011/2012 parliamentary elections. EEW provides readers with a wealth of information and analysis on the major actors and institutions that made up these elections, as well as a close view into Egypt's "new" political arena. The project did not take for granted the notion that these are truly competitive elections equally accessible to all important social forces in Egypt, and featuring serious candidates and real political parties with meaningful agendas and coherent political platforms. Therefore, where relevant, EEW researchers have sought to highlight tensions and flaws challenging such a view, in the interest of providing readers with a nuanced insight into Egypt's electoral arena.

Based on extensive research and interviews, EEW's profile entries are divided into four main sections: (1) Parties; (2) Coalitions; (3) Figures and Actors; and (4) Laws and Processes. A final section summarizes the election results for the lower house of parliament.

Parties

In this section, EEW overviews the important political groups and electoral coalitions that participated in the 2011/2012 elections. Also included in the section are profiles for parties that decided to boycott the parliamentary poll, but whose presence in the political arena is worthy of attention. Readers will also find information on the major political parties that are believed to represent some of the elements and factions that once constituted the former ruling National Democratic Party (NDP), which was dissolved by court order in April 2011.

Each political party profile is meant to give readers a detailed view into the party's political history and (if relevant) the various political trends and factions constituting the organization, its plans for parliamentary elections, its positions on salient political matters, its alliances and relationships with other members of the political community, and the most important figures associated with the party.

While many parties identified themselves during the lead-up to the elections as agents of the January 25 Revolution and long-standing anti-Mubarak activists, the sub-section "Before the Revolution" brings to light realities that do not always bode well with the self-narrated histories of these groups, along with their self-professed "revolutionary credentials."

The sub-section on "Parliamentary Elections" is meant to give a summary of how many seats each party contested, and who their most prominent candidates were. It is notable to observe that the majority of parties that have been able to present candidates for more than ninety percent of the available seats in parliament are either traditional opposition forces that Egypt inherited from the Mubarak era (e.g., Al-Wafd Party and the Muslim Brotherhood-led Democratic Alliance for Egypt), political groups allied with big business interests (e.g., Egyptian Bloc electoral coalition led by Naguib Sawiris's Free Egyptians Party), Salafist groups suspected of receiving enormous amounts of foreign funds (e.g., the Islamist Bloc led by Al-Nour Party), parties dominated by former NDP members, or some combination of all of the above. Left-leaning parties that do not cater to any of the aforementioned interests struggled to field a comparable number of candidates through their electoral rosters. The Revolution Continues Alliance, which featured the Socialist Popular Alliance Party (SPA) and the now-dissolved Revolution's Youth Coalition (RYC) as well as others, is a case in point. It competed for no more than sixty percent of the parliament's lower house.

The sub-section on "Relationship with Other Political Parties" highlights a given party's most significant electoral alliances and rivalries, and its affiliation, if any, with Egypt's major electoral coalitions. The sub-section on "Stances on Salient Issues" summarizes each party's positions on important policy questions. It includes an explanation of each party's understanding of social justice, along with its vision for improving the country's economic conditions. This sub-section also includes a discussion of a given party's position on the role of religion in the affairs of the state, foreign relations, particularly vis-à-vis the United States and the Arab-Israeli conflict, military trials of civilians, and labor strikes.

In compiling this information, EEW researchers did not simply defer to each party's written platform. Instead, they attempted to reach out to party leaders, and assessed the consistency of their official positions with their actions and inactions. Inconsistencies and ambiguities were not sidelined. In fact, they were highlighted.

Coalitions

In this section, EEW offers a fuller and more detailed profile of the four largest electoral coalitions, namely the Democratic Alliance for Egypt, the Egyptian Bloc, the Islamist Bloc, and the Revolution Continues Alliance (RCA). One important trend is worth highlighting: these coalitions were mostly based on unequal partnerships, whereby a resourceful "sponsor" dominated the electoral lists of each alliance. That sponsor is the Muslim Brotherhood's Freedom and Justice Party (FJP) in the case of the Democratic Alliance, the Free Egyptians Party (albeit to a lesser extent) in the Egyptian Bloc, and Al-Nour Party in the Islamist Bloc.

This pattern partly reflects asymmetries in the financial resources and electoral experiences across parties. It also mirrors the strong interest of certain actors, like the Muslim Brotherhood, in portraying their potential electoral gains as the outcome of a broad national consensus that travels beyond a single group, as opposed to an attempt to single-handedly dominate the electoral arena at the exclusion of others. Whether or not the Democratic Alliance—wherein the FJP dominated the candidate rosters while the coalition's other parties got the "leftovers"—does in fact represent a "broad national consensus" is open to interpretation. However, its very existence reveals a great deal about how the Brotherhood would like to be perceived.

Finally, the asymmetrical nature of these alliances also underscores the dominance of parochial interests among many Egyptian parties. The abundance of parties that agreed to bargains limiting their own electoral prospects to a handful of parliamentary seats suggests that, for many parties in Egypt today, the narrow objective of getting a few good men elected is taking precedence over the need to represent meaningful national agendas that travel across more than just a few districts. The latter observation could not be more pertinent given widespread assertions that once protest movements demobilize, party life and elected legislatures in Egypt would step up to the plate and pick up where these movements have left off in terms of advancing important national political and economic reform agendas.

Figures and Actors

While each political party profile includes short biographies of key party officials and associates, the section entitled "Figures and Actors" expands on some of these short summaries to provide fuller profiles of these individuals. The section also offers profiles of individuals who are not currently occupying official leadership positions inside legal political parties, but who are shaping Egyptian politics in meaningful ways. The purpose of this section is not to provide an exhaustive list of Egyptian politicians and activists. Rather, the goal is to offer a set of illustrative examples of emerging activists who are seeking to carve a role for themselves in the political arena, along with examples of traditional politicians who are struggling to reinvent themselves to survive in a changing political environment. The latter trend has taken many shapes and forms, going as far as former NDP leaders posing as supporters of the revolution.

Laws and Processes

The section on "Laws and Processes" summarizes the major rules and processes that governed the 2011/2012 parliamentary elections. Egypt's electoral field is subject to a number of laws and frameworks that govern the powers of various state branches and agencies, the formation of political parties, the exercise of political rights, and the powers of the parliament and the method of its election. "The Concise Idiot's Guide to the Egyptian Elections" overviews the most basic relevant rules and regulations, including dates for voting (and run-offs) in each governorate, number of constituencies, and electoral systems.

Results

The election results section provides a summary of the final breakdown of seats by party/coalition in the People's Assembly in the immediate aftermath of the election. It also includes a full listing of elected members of the parliament's lower house, along with the district or governorate they represent, their party affiliation, and their corresponding type of membership (professional, labor, or *fellah*).

Collectively, all these sections offer observers and students of Egypt an invaluable guide to understanding the post-January 25 Egyptian political field, as well as the major institutions and actors who are shaping it.

1 | Parties

AL-ADL PARTY

Al-Adl Party was formally established in the wake of former president Hosni Mubarak's ouster. The party declares that it seeks to protect the goals of Egypt's January 25 Revolution and promote the country's social and economic development. Al-Adl professes a liberal platform calling for a civil, free, and modern state, though the party decided from the outset not to align itself with Egypt's secular or Islamist camps, calling instead for a "third way."

Before the Revolution

Its main founding member, Mustafa Al-Naggar, is a former member of the Muslim Brotherhood (MB) and a current member of the Revolution's Youth Coalition. Al-Naggar has played an active role in the National Association for Change, a reform movement led by former United Nations official Mohamed ElBaradei. The Association is a coalition of opposition figures and groups that formed in 2010 to demand democratic reforms, as well as free and fair presidential elections in which independent candidates can run without being handpicked by the regime. Al-Naggar actively participated in Egypt's January 25 Revolution, specifically in the eighteen-day Tahrir Square sit-in that ultimately led to Mubarak's exit.

Al-Adl Party logo. Image from face-book.com/aladlparty.

Al-Naggar describes Al-Adl, which he co-founded following Mubarak's resignation, as a party that offers Egyptians a centrist alternative to the Brotherhood, one guided by an effort to move beyond longstanding ideological rivalries that characterize Egyptian politics. Al-Adl, according to another founding member, represents a midway point between liberal and religious parties.

While Al-Adl Party participated in several "million-person" rallies after Mubarak's ouster, during the lead up to the 2011/2012 elections the party shifted its focus to electoral campaigning and providing social services to low-income communities.

Party Structure

Tasked with running the party is a supreme council, which includes the party chair, the secretary general, fifty members directly elected by the General Assembly, chairs of party organizations, representatives of governorate branches, and the party's nationally-elected members of parliament. Both the party chair and secretary general are elected by the General Assembly comprised by governorate office members, the chairs of party organizations (e.g., women's and youth organizations), and function-based committees (e.g. advisory, media, health, and education committees). Al-Adl has branches in every Egyptian village or city where more than twenty party members reside. Governorate branches include all elected village- and city-branch members.

Parliamentary Elections

In parliamentary polls, Al-Adl Party fielded a total of 195 candidates (out of a possible 678) in eighteen governorates for both the upper and lower houses of parliament. Through eighteen lists (out of a possible forty-six), Al-Adl fielded 144 party-list candidates (out of a possible 332) for the parliament's lower house, in addition to twenty-three candidates for individual candidacy races (out of a possible 166). Through five lists (out of a possible thirty), Al-Adl fielded twenty party-list candidates (out of a possible 120), and eight candidates (out of a possible sixty) for the upper house of parliament's individual candidacy races. In total, there were 678 parliamentary seats up for election (498 in the lower house and 180 in the upper house). The legal framework that governed the 2011/2012 parliamentary elections gave SCAF the right to appoint ten of the 508 members of the lower house, and ninety of the 270 members of the upper house.

Relationship with Other Political Parties

Al-Adl Party announced it would participate in the 2011/2012 elections independently of major alliances. Distancing itself from electoral coalitions, both secular and Islamist, Al-Adl chose instead to propose the creation of The Third Path: The Egyptian Centrist Movement, a platform that sought to unite Egypt's political forces and transcend traditional Islamist-secular divides. This initiative, however, never materialized, and Al-Adl Party remains largely independent.

When the MB-led Democratic Alliance and the secular-leaning Egyptian Bloc were formed, Al-Adl Party refused to commit to either coalition. Al-Adl, however, was briefly a member of the Democratic Alliance. The party withdrew from this coalition early, on the grounds that it would not cooperate with traditional opposition groups that were loyal to the previous regime and that benefited from its largesse. The alliance contained several parties that were pejoratively dubbed "paper parties" during the Mubarak era, in reference to the insignificance of their roles.

Stances on Salient Issues

Form of Government

According to its platform, Al-Adl Party believes in a "mixed" system of government that combines elements of presidential and parliamentary democracy based on separation of powers and executive accountability to the legislature.

Economic Policy

Party officials say they want to build an economic system that guarantees social justice and development by giving a vibrant role to the private sector and limiting state intervention. Al-Adl Party encourages cooperation between public and private sectors to advance and manage major infrastructure projects.

The party aims to achieve national economic development by providing investment incentives, supporting scientific research and development, and investing in human resources. Egypt's economic system, the party stresses, should be decentralized, transparent, and accountable so as to prevent corruption and monopolistic practices.

Al-Adl also calls for using Egypt's natural resources in an environmentally friendly way and endorses greater reliance on renewable energy.

Social Justice

The party describes "social justice" as one of its fundamental guiding principles. Under this rubric, it proposes the introduction of a minimum wage for public sector employees, progressive taxes not to exceed thirty five percent, and tax exemptions for low-income households. Al-Adl's "social justice" platform, however, falls short of also endorsing a minimum wage in the private sector.

Al-Adl calls for lifting price subsidies. The party proposes, instead, that government cash subsidies be distributed directly to relevant recipients. Such a policy, according to Al-Adl, would ensure that subsidies reach communities who need them most.

Religion and Politics

According to its party program, Al-Adl Party adopts a centrist position, attempting to strike a balance between values associated with modern civil states and Egyptian society's religious and cultural values.

Al-Adl Party endorses Article 2 of Egypt's constitution, which states that Islam is the primary source of legislation in Egypt. The party also upholds the freedom of belief and religious practice to the extent by which they do not infringe on others' rights. Al-Adl further supports human rights as expressed by international conventions and religious principles, and it calls for freedom of expression for all citizens.

Al-Adl embraces the concept of citizenship, which holds that all Egyptians are equal before the law, regardless of religion, gender, race, or class. All citizens, the party believes, should enjoy equal opportunity vis-à-vis government employment and state appointments.

Strike Law and Labor Movements

Last June 2011, Al-Adl founder Mustafa Al-Naggar described the law banning strikes and demonstrations as "unacceptable" and called for the independence of labor unions and professional syndicates to help guarantee an active and effective civil society.

Military Trials

Al-Adl Party opposes the practice of referring civilian suspects to military trials and has condemned military prosecution of political activists. Al-Adl participated in the 9 September 2011 Tahrir demonstration entitled "Correcting the Path," which was organized partly to protest the use of military trials by Egyptian authorities. The party also opposes all forms of torture and upholds each citizen's right to privacy in all spheres of life.

Foreign Relations

Al-Adl Party proclaims a commitment to a foreign policy based on internationally accepted values of human rights, justice, and freedom. Regarding the Palestinian issue, the party platform states its support for all relevant international agreements and resolutions. It also supports Palestinians' right to self-determination and to an independent state with Jerusalem as its capital. Al-Adl opposes any normalization of relations with Israel until it returns the Palestinian occupied territories and ceases hostilities against Palestinians.

Media Image and Controversies

The party witnessed mass resignations shortly after its establishment in late 2011. There were speculations that these resignations happened because of allegations that party leaders allowed former members of Mubarak's now-defunct National Democratic Party into Al-Adl. Some commentators attributed these resignations to revelations that the party was receiving funds from famous businessman Hisham Al-Khazindar, managing director of Egypt's largest private equity fund, Citadel Capital.

Since its establishment, Al-Adl Party has participated in several meetings with SCAF to discuss the parliamentary elections and other issues. The party again suffered internal ruptures after one meeting when Al-Naggar agreed to sign a highly contentious SCAF statement with thirteen other parties. The document implicitly upheld the extension of longstanding emergency laws and the practice of referring civilian suspects to military courts, although it offered parties some concessions related to election laws. Critics inside Al-Adl saw the document as a deadly compromise, because, in addition to upholding the aforementioned measures, it committed signatories to fully support SCAF as protector of the revolution and leader of Egypt's transitional period.

In response, several Al-Adl Party members issued an official statement criticizing Al-Naggar for his decision. Shortly afterward, Al-Naggar declared that he had revoked his signature on the document, adding that he would leave it up to the party's General Assembly to decide whether or not to commit the party to the statement. When the party's General Assembly put the issue to a vote, a majority nevertheless agreed to endorse the controversial SCAF document.

Key Figures

Mustafa Al-Naggar

A founding member of Al-Adl Party, Mustafa Al-Naggar was born in Alexandria in 1980. He has a Bachelor's Degree in dentistry and a degree in mass communication from Cairo University and the American University in Cairo, respectively.

Al-Naggar hails from a family with traditional MB sympathies, and he himself became a member of the group's youth wing, although he left it in 2005. Since his withdrawal from the Brotherhood, Al-Naggar has embraced a more "centrist" approach to Egyptian politics, which has largely become the foundation for Al-Adl Party.

Al-Naggar also played an active role in the National Association for Change reform movement. In 2010, Al-Naggar's online human rights advocacy earned him an honorary award from the United Nations High Commissioner on Refugees in Beirut, and at one point he served as coordinator for the Arab Journalists and Bloggers Network for Human Rights.

Al-Naggar actively participated in Egypt's January 25 Revolution from the outset and was present for the eighteen-day Tahrir Square sit-in that ultimately led to Mubarak's ouster.

Amr Al-Shobaki

A writer and political analyst, Amr Al-Shobaki is a founding member of Al-Adl and is currently a member of the party's Advisory Committee. Al-Shobaki graduated from Cairo University with a degree in political science in 1984 and obtained a doctorate in political science from France's Sorbonne University in 2001.

An expert in domestic Egyptian politics and Islamist political movements, he currently works at the Cairo-based Al-Ahram Center for Political and Strategic Studies and is the managing editor of *Ahwal Mesreya* (Egyptian Affairs) magazine.

He is also the president of the Arab Forum of Alternatives, an organization that promotes democratic culture.

Al-Shobaki ran in Egypt's 2011 parliamentary polls for an individual candidacy seat in the Giza governorate.

Mona ElBaradei

A former chairperson of Cairo University's Department of Economics, Mona ElBaradei is one of Al-Adl Party's most prominent members. She is the sister of former UN official and prominent Egyptian political leader Mohamed ElBaradei. She currently serves as president of the Egyptian National Council for Enhancing Competitiveness.

Mona ElBaradei calls for greater transparency in Egyptian policymaking, arguing that the absence of such transparency discourages foreign investment. She strongly criticizes the Mubarak regime for its tendency to focus on economic growth, while ignoring the issue of income distribution. She has consistently called for encouraging small Egyptian businesses and projects. She is also a proponent of setting national minimum and maximum public-sector wages.

Mona ElBaradei was an avid supporter of her brother's 2010 campaign for constitutional reform and backed his bid for the presidency.

DEMOCRATIC WORKERS' PARTY

The Democratic Workers' Party (DWP) was founded by former members of the Revolutionary Socialists and other labor activists right after the ouster of Hosni Mubarak in February 2011.

DWP's main aim has been to defend labor rights and press for better working conditions. In addition to labor activists, party membership includes students and farmers.

During Mubarak's last decade of rule, Egypt witnessed a sharp increase in workers' strikes, most notably the Mahalla Strike of 2006. That year, more than 20,000 textile workers went on strike in the city of Mahalla, one of Egypt's biggest industrial cities, to protest management's refusal to pay them a two-month profit bonus. The Mahalla workers attempted to initiate another mass strike in 2008, but their attempt was violently aborted after fierce clashes with state security forces. Subsequently, the entire city of Mahalla rebelled, and protesters started tearing down pictures of Hosni Mubarak.

The increase in labor strikes furthered the formation of independent trade unions as an alternative to state-dominated trade unions. Real Estate Tax Collectors were the first civil servants to establish an independent trade union in December 2008.

Democratic Workers' Party logo. Image from al-Ma-shad.com

Additionally, workers' strikes were essential in setting the stage for the January 25 Revolution. The growing wave of strikes after 2006 eventually led many opposition groups to focus their efforts on demanding an increase in the legal minimum wage from thirty-five EGP (no more than seven dollars per month) to 1,200 EGP. Their efforts ultimately led to a 2010 administrative court ruling upholding their demand, insisting the government implement the increase.

The DWP aims to be a voice for Egyptian workers who seek better pay and working conditions, as well as an improved social security program. Many workers who had been active in labor movements during Mubarak's rule have joined the party together with members of the Revolutionary Socialists, a Trotskyite group known for its support of the labor movement.

Before the Revolution

The Revolutionary Socialists played a notable role in supporting workers' strikes and demands before the January 25 Revolution. Originally established in 1995 by student groups active since the late 1980s, the Revolutionary Socialists has been influenced by Trotskyism and defines itself as an anti-capitalist group seeking to attain a socialist society through revolutionary change. The group believes this

change should be global and should not be limited to any one country.

Though initially confined to university and intellectual settings, Revolutionary Socialists took to the streets during the second Palestinian Intifada and joined forces with the Egyptian Popular Committee in Solidarity with the Intifada. The Revolutionary Socialists have taken part in many coalitions since, and its members participated as individual members in the 2005 Kefaya movement. During the years preceding the January 25 Revolution, the group focused primarily on supporting the demands of worker social movements, particularly calls to set the monthly minimum wage to 1,200 EGP.

During the lead-up to the elections, the DWP participated in all major demonstrations and sit-ins organized in Tahrir Square, including the three-week 8 July 2011 sit-in, which was forcefully dispersed on 1 August 2011 by Egyptian police, military, and security forces. The DWP continues to support workers' strikes and the fight against the ban on labor strikes and demonstrations. Additionally, the DWP has supported efforts to establish independent trade unions.

Party Structure

The DWP lacks a hierarchical structure, and is comprised of different committees. The Policymaking Committee is responsible for developing the party's program goals and policy strategy with input from party members. The Public Actions Committee is responsible for establishing links with workers engaged in strikes in Egypt and supporting their demands. An Organizational Committee receives and processes membership applications. It also collects subscriptions and donations. The Media Committee is tasked with formulating public statements in partnership with the Policymaking Committee. It also manages the DWP Facebook page, Sawt Al-Omal (Workers' Voice).

The Organizational Committee is concerned with receiving and processing membership applications, and collecting subscriptions and donations. A Task Management Committee is responsible for overseeing and coordinating activities of the party's affiliated labor groups, including groups active in factories or companies in various parts of the country. The Committee for Reclaiming Privatized Companies is responsible for collecting signatures in support of reversing the privatization of public sector companies. The committee includes several lawyers who are taking legal action relevant to this initiative.

The DWP is currently focusing on activating enough workers' groups across the country in order to hold internal elections and form a Founding Committee, which will contain five members from each location.

Parliamentary Elections

While there were disagreements within the party on whether or not to participate, the party ultimately decided to boycott the legislative election process. Kamal Khalil, a key DWP political leader, told *Jadaliyya/Ahram Online* that the party does not approve of the current political environment in which elections were scheduled to take place because emergency and anti-strike laws remained in effect, while thousands of civilians were facing military trials. The DWP is one of two leftist parties that decided to boycott the parliamentary poll, the second being the Egyptian Communist Party.

Relationship with Other Political Parties

The DWP's cooperation with other political parties is limited. But it has close ties to trade unions and like-minded social movements, notably the Independent Federation of Trade Unions, Popular Committees for the Defense of the Revolution, and the Revolutionary Socialists.

Stances on Salient Issues

Economic Policy, Social Justice, and Labor

The DWP calls for a minimum wage of 1,500 EGP per month and a maximum wage of 30,000 EGP per month for state employees and workers. It also calls for all state pensions to be at least 1,200 EGP per month and adjusted regularly with inflation. The party also seeks to establish a national scheme for unemployment benefits of at least 600 EGP per month and is also involved in promoting independent trade unions.

The DWP also supports nationalization, without compensation, of all public sector companies sold to private investors at below market price—whether foreign or local. The party further calls for nationalizing companies crucial to agriculture, including companies involved in the production and distribution of water and the production of seeds and fertilizers. It also calls for an abolition of all outstanding farmer debts.

The DWP opposes healthcare privatization projects and supports the nationalization of all major hospitals. The party calls for free health care and education for all Egyptians and urges a substantial increase in Egypt's healthcare budget.

Minorities

The DWP is committed to the equality of all individuals irrespective of religion, gender, ethnicity, or race. It supports a constitution that upholds a civil democratic state that protects the economic and social rights of all its citizens.

Military Trials and Strike Laws

The DWP opposes the military trials of civilians, the emergency law, and the law criminalizing strikes, demonstrations, and sit-ins. It has participated in several protests against these practices and laws, and has signed statements denouncing them.

Foreign Relations

The DWP calls for annulling Egypt's peace treaty with Israel. The party opposes normalization and any form of cooperation with Israel.

Media Image and Controversies

Although the DWP stands for what can be labeled as socialist ideals, many workers within its membership refuse to be labeled as such. Thus, the party does not officially identify itself as a socialist party.

A heated debate took place within the party's membership on whether or not it should boycott the parliamentary elections. While most workers wanted the party to participate in the elections, the "Revolutionary Socialists" wing inside the party favored a boycott. The party ultimately decided to boycott the poll.

Key Figures

Haitham Mohammadein

Haitham Mohammadein is a revolutionary socialist, a human rights lawyer affiliated with the Nadim Center for the Rehabilitation of Victims of Violence, and a member of the Independent Federation of Trade Unions.

Kamal Khalil

Kamal Khalil used to be a student activist and member of the January 8 Organization, a Marxist group active during the 1970s which later merged with the Communist Labor Party to form the Labor Party in 1983. He was arrested for instigating unrest during the 1977 bread riots.

Khalil joined the Revolutionary Socialists in 1990, then resigned after the organization split into two different groups: the Revolutionary Socialists and the Socialist Renewal Current. He says that he resigned to make room for younger activists to take on leadership positions. Khalil is also one of the founders of the Kefaya movement and a member of Democratic Engineers, a political group active with the Egyptian Engineers' Syndicate.

Khalil is known for his leading role in street demonstrations and was arrested by state security more than fifteen times. He participated in several anti-war and anti-Zionist initiatives and demonstrations.

Born in 1949, Khalil holds an engineering degree from Cairo University.

Kamal Al-Fayyumi

A founder of the Democratic Workers' Party, Kamal Al-Fayyumi has been a worker at the Mahalla Textile Factory since the age of eighteen. He participated in the 2006 Mahalla Strike and subsequently represented workers in negotiations with the General Union of Textile Workers. Al-Fayyumi was one of the organizers of the 6 April 2008 General Strike, which led to his abduction and detention by the Egyptian State Security Investigation Services.

Egyptian Current Party

The Egyptian Current Party is one of many political parties founded in the wake of former president Hosni Mubarak's ouster. Many of its leading members formerly belonged to the Muslim Brotherhood's youth wing and the April 6 youth movement, along with several independent young activists involved in the January 25 Revolution.

Before the Revolution

The April 6 Movement played a prominent role in the political efforts that ultimately led to the 25 January 2011 uprising, organizing a number of anti-Mubarak marches and demonstrations. The movement eventually split into two wings: the Ahmed Maher Front and the Democratic Front.

The split initially surfaced when some leaders inside the movement announced plans to turn the April 6 Movement into an NGO or foundation rather than an unofficial political movement. After some members claimed they were not consulted in that decision, subsequent fissures emerged due to concerns about the lack of transparency and inclusive deliberation in the movement's decision-making process. Both wings of the movement oppose the idea of turning April 6 into a political party, preferring to maintain its role as a pressure group aimed at lobbying the government to implement key demands of the revolution.

The youth wing of the Muslim Brotherhood (MB) participated in the 25 January demonstrations, even though its leadership refused to endorse these efforts initially. During the eighteen-day Tahrir Square sit-in, which paved the way for Mubarak's exit, the MB's youth wing played a major role in protecting protesters from regime-hired thugs.

Following the formation of the Egyptian Current Party, which some of the Brotherhood's youth co-founded, considerable tensions grew between the group and the MB. Brotherhood leaders had threatened to expel any members who join any political party other than the Freedom and Justice Party and identified the Egyptian Current Party by name in its directive.

According to a MB member who was expelled in the wake of this incident, the group witnessed mass expulsions following the launch of the Egyptian Current Party. These developments coincided with resignations from senior MB figures, including Abdel Moneim Abul Futtoh and former deputy supreme guide Mohamed Habib.

Some say that disagreements within the Brotherhood were the result of differences in political strategy inside the group. Mohamed Osman, a former MB activist, says that some Brotherhood members, especially among its youth, believe in deep transformative change, while the group's leaders seem to espouse a more conservative vision for reform. The advent of the revolutionary change in Egypt exacerbated these differences, hence reports of fissures inside the group following Mubarak's ouster.

Several of the Egyptian Current's main founders were also members of the now-dissolved Revolution's Youth Coalition (RYC), which included some of the MB's youth and affiliates of the April 6 Movement. MB youth who joined the Egyptian Current were expelled from the group. As Brotherhood members, these activists had called for greater coordination between the MB and non-Islamist political factions.

Party Structure

A twenty member supreme council is tasked with running the party. The council includes the party's founding members, in addition to eight elected members. The party boasts several specialized sub-committees, including committees for media affairs, party activities, fundraising, and subscriptions.

Parliamentary Elections

The Egyptian Current contested the parliamentary elections through the Revolution Continues electoral alliance. The coalition includes the Revolution's Youth Coalition, the Socialist Popular Alliance, the Free Egypt Party, the Egyptian Socialist Party, the Equality and Development Party, and the Egyptian Alliance Party.

Through 280 candidates (out of a possible 332), the RCA contested thirty-four (out of a possible forty-six) party list races for the 508-member lower house of parliament. Additionally, twenty-six (out of a possible 166) candidates contested individual candidacy race seats. The legal framework that governed the 2011/2012 parliamentary elections gave SCAF the right to appoint ten of the 508 members of the lower house, and ninety of the 270 members of the upper house.

According to Egyptian Current Party leader and former Muslim Brotherhood member Islam Lotfy, 100 of these candidates are below the age of forty. The majority of candidates that the alliance fielded belong to the SPA, according to RCA member Khaled Abdel Hamid. Some thirty-two are affiliates of the Egyptian Current Party. Prominent party activists who ran in the election include party cofounders, Islam Lotfy, Asmaa Mahfouz, and Mohamed Al-Qasas.

Titled "Security, Freedom, and Social Justice," the RCA's platform, which it announced in early November 2011, focused on re-establishing law and order, promoting social justice, and closing the income gap between the rich and the poor. It also called for securing a swift transfer of power from the ruling military council to an elected civilian authority by mid-2012.

Relationship with Other Political Parties

The Egyptian Current has had a tense relationship with the MB, since it is largely responsible for instigating a significant split within the Brotherhood, which barred its members from joining the Egyptian Current Party.

Egyptian Current Party members were also part of the now-dissolved Revolution's Youth Coalition (RYC), and therefore closely coordinated their activities with the group, as well as organizations with members linked to the RYC, such as the Socialist

Popular Alliance and the Justice and Freedom Movement.

The party is a member of the Revolution Continues electoral coalition, which, according to its members, comprises an ideologically diverse set of political actors, namely liberals, Islamists, and socialists.

Stances on Salient Issues

Social Justice and Economic Policy

The party's vision is a developmental one, and sees its role as raising political awareness and cooperating with civil society in the pursuit of national projects that would improve the socio-economic conditions of workers, farmers, students, professors, and all other segments of society.

The party aims to promote a democratic transition in Egypt in line with the desires and needs of the Egyptian people. It aims to empower the politically, economically, and socially marginalized, including women and the disabled.

The party supports the notion of citizenship, meaning that all citizens should enjoy equal rights. It also supports the inclusion of Egyptians living and working abroad in the country's political life.

The Egyptian Current supports enhancing public services offered to citizens. It believes in every individual's right to equal opportunity in accessing education, healthcare and housing. It aims to eradicate poverty through job creation and unemployment benefits.

The party further believes that development should also include minimizing the gender gap in education, employment, and leading government positions. It supports a fair and equal distribution of national wealth and public services. It advocates for investing Egypt's academic and professional resources in planning and managing the country's development projects. It stresses the importance of labor-intensive projects and small and medium enterprises.

Religion and State

The party is not concerned with the burgeoning political polarization between secular and Islamist forces, believing that this division is not reflective of traditional Egyptian society, says party member Mohamed Osman.

The Egyptian Current Party sees Egypt's identity as stemming from its Arab, African, and Islamic roots.

The party has vocally criticized the role of Egyptian media in fostering an atmosphere of sectarian animosity. It released a statement condemning the 9 October 2011 attack by military police on Coptic demonstrators that left at least twenty-five dead and hundreds injured.

Military Trials

The Egyptian Current also took a strong stance against the practice of trying civilian suspects in military courts. One of their founding members, former April 6 member Asmaa Mahfouz, faced military prosecution for her public criticism of Egypt's ruling military council and had to be bailed out of prison for 20,000 EGP (3,355 USD).

Strike Law and Labor Movements

The party supports workers' rights to wage labor strikes in demand of better working conditions.

Foreign Relations

According to party member Mohamed Osman, the party believes that Egypt should seek to achieve complete national political and economic independence from outside powers. It opposes all forms of foreign intervention in Egypt, and believes in the right of the Palestinian people to nationhood, self-determination, and the pursuit of all forms of resistance against the Israeli occupation.

Media Image and Controversies

The Egyptian Current Party is often portrayed in the media as the party that disaffected Muslim Brotherhood youth founded, although a number of its members originally hail from other political youth movements as well.

The media spotlight was cast on the nascent party when founding member Asmaa Mahfouz was accused of inciting violence against the Egyptian Armed Forces, a charge for which she was brought before a military tribunal. The charge was later dropped.

Along with the RYC, the Egyptian Current Party almost withdrew from the RCA one week before the candidate registration deadline, objecting that the SPA was dominating the top positions of all lists at the expense of the youth groups. The problem was quickly renegotiated to allow more youth members to head lists.

Key Figures

Mohamed Al-Qasas

Born in 1974, Mohamed Al-Qasas is a founding member of the Egyptian Current Party and serves on its supreme council. He is a former MB member and had been a leading figure in the movement's youth wing.

After the January 25 Revolution, Al-Qasas spearheaded the campaign to establish other MB parties aside from the Freedom and Justice Party – a position for which he was ultimately expelled from the Brotherhood.

Prior to his expulsion, Al-Qasas also clashed with the MB leadership when he, along with others, refused to pull out of the now-dissolved Revolution's Youth Coalition when it began adopting positions with which the Brotherhood disagreed. After Mubarak's ouster, MB youth affiliated with the RYC, including Al-Qasas, supported the Coalition's decision to organize and participate in Tahrir Square demonstrations that the Brotherhood's senior leadership officially boycotted.

Al-Qasas had also been part of a Brotherhood youth movement that had called for greater cooperation with non-Islamist political groups. This same movement supported several important demands largely overlooked by the MB's senior leadership, including workers' rights to strike. The MB youth faction also tended to be more critical than their leaders of the military's role in managing Egypt's post-Mubarak political affairs.

Al-Qasas ran parliamentary polls on the party's list in the Cairo district of Heliopolis.

Asmaa Mahfouz

A founding member of the Egyptian Current Party, Asmaa Mahfouz is a former leading member of the April 6 youth movement and was a member of the now-dissolved Revolution's Youth Coalition. Before the revolution, as an April 6 member, she organized and participated in a number of anti-Mubarak demonstrations and marches.

Mahfouz was born in 1985 and graduated from Cairo University with a degree in business. In the parliamentary election, she contested an individual candidacy race seat in the Cairo district of Heliopolis.

Islam Lotfy

Islam Lotfy is a founding member of the Egyptian Current and currently serves on the party's supreme council. He previously belonged to the Muslim Brotherhood before getting expelled, along with several colleagues, when he took part in founding the Egyptian Current.

A former member of the now-dissolved Revolution's Youth Coalition, Lotfy ran as a candidate on the party's list in Giza's 6th of October district.

EGYPTIAN SOCIAL DEMOCRATIC PARTY

The Egyptian Social Democratic Party was founded in the wake of Egypt's January 25 Revolution. Officially launched in March 2011, the party combines several groups sharing a liberal and social democratic outlook that were politically active in the years preceding the revolution.

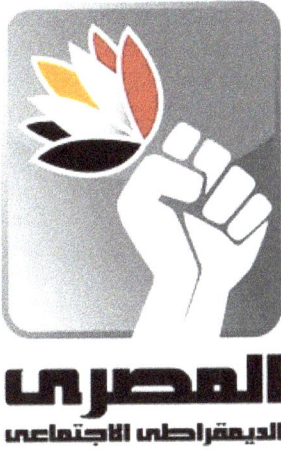

Egyptian Social Democratic Party logo. Image from egysdp.com.

These groups include individuals who, prior to the revolution, were involved in an unsuccessful attempt to form a center-left party known as the Social Democratic Party. Two prominent members, Farid Zahran and Ziad Al-Elaimy, participated in Mohamed Abul-Ghar's March 9 Movement for the Independence of Universities. The two other groups are members of Mohamed ElBaradei's National Association for Change and the leftist Justice and Freedom youth movement.

The party's founding members include Abul-Ghar and Zahran and Hazem Beblawi, an economist and former UN official who also served as deputy prime minister in the government of Essam Sharaf. Other founding members include political analyst and activist Amr Hamzawy, who later left the party in protest of a statement it issued condemning the military personnel's use of violence against Tahrir Square demonstrators on 9 April 2011. Hamzawy opposed this statement and complained he was not consulted in its drafting.

The Egyptian Social Democratic Party espouses a social democratic vision, staunchly upholding democratic ideals in politics, the economy, and society. The party emphasizes the need to support labor within a free market system. Founding member Farid Zahran once said: "I cannot have a social democratic party without having a businessman and a union representative side by side."

The party unequivocally calls for a secular state. Abul Ghar asserted at the outset, "Our paramount concern is having a secular country."

Members insist that the party is neither strictly liberal nor leftist. Instead, many supporters contend that the Egyptian Social Democratic Party represents the combination of reform-minded leftists and market-oriented liberals. Members also say that the party is modeled after social democratic groups found in Scandinavia and some Latin American countries, such as Brazil.

The diversity of political and economic orientations in the party may limit its cohesion in the future. "We need the strength of a big party that brings together leftist and liberal forces to build a democracy," said democratic leftist party member Bassam Mortada. "But two years or so from now, we might diverge into different parties."

Before the Revolution

The party's founding members include a number of activists who played a political role before and during the revolution, as well as professionals and artists who had been critical of former president Hosni Mubarak's regime.

Founding member Ziad Al-Eleimy, veteran activist and close associate of opposition leader Mohamed ElBaradei, played a leading role in the now-dissolved Revolution's Youth Coalition. This loose grouping of youth-oriented opposition movements emerged during the eighteen-day uprising in 2011. Abul-Ghar, one of the party's founding members, served as a spokesperson for the National Association for Change. In 2010, the National Association for Change called for democratic reforms such as free and fair presidential elections allowing independent candidates—like Mohamed ElBaradei—to run without being handpicked by the Mubarak regime.

Party Structure

The Egyptian Social Democratic Party's bylaws provide for the election of all its bodies, including the party's highest executive authority, the supreme council. The supreme council is responsible for making decisions on behalf of the party in consultation with the party chair.

Parliamentary Elections

The Egyptian Social Democratic Party contested the election through the Egyptian Bloc coalition, which fielded parliamentary candidates on a unified list. The Egyptian Bloc fielded 412 candidates for parliamentary lower house elections. The bloc contested all 332 party list seats available in the 508-member lower house, in addition to fielding eighty (out of a possible 166) candidates for individual candidacy races. The legal framework that governed the 2011/2012 parliamentary elections gave SCAF the right to appoint ten of the 508 members of the lower house.

Half of the candidates are affiliated with the Free Egyptians Party, forty percent with the Egyptian Social Democratic Party, and ten percent with the Al-Tagammu Party.

Under the slogan "together, we will achieve what is ours," the Egyptian Bloc's campaign underscored the goals of building a civil democratic state and promoting economic prosperity through a liberal economy committed to social justice. For many observers, it is unclear how the unlikely partnership between the Free Egyptians Party, known for its pro-business orientations, and the socialist Al-Tagammu could possibly yield a meaningful, joint vision for Egypt's economy in the future. Since its inception, Al-Tagammu has sought to fight economic liberalization, as well as many other aspects of the economic vision espoused by the Free Egyptians.

Relationship with Other Political Parties

The Egyptian Social Democratic Party joined forces with fourteen other groups in August 2011 to create the Egyptian Bloc, an electoral coalition of liberal and leftist forces. The coalition once consisted of twenty-one groups, including the leftist Popular Socialist Alliance Party, the liberal Free Egypt Party, the Free Egyptians Party, the Popular Worker's Union, and the National Association for Change. After successive defections, three parties remained: the Egyptian Social Democratic Party, the Free Egyptians Party, and the leftist Al-Tagammu Party. Some defecting groups accused fellow Egyptian Bloc members of fielding candidates who were once affiliated with the now-defunct National Democratic Party, an allegation that the Egyptian Bloc's spokespeople deny. Others complained that candidate selection processes lacked transparency.

While some contend that the Egyptian Bloc was primarily formed to counterbalance the threat posed by the Democratic Alliance, a rival coalition spearheaded by the influential and well-organized Muslim Brotherhood (MB), the Egyptian Bloc's party founder Abul-Ghar insists otherwise. Abul-Ghar contends that the Egyptian Bloc was not created to oppose any particular political force, stressing that Islamists were welcome to join the coalition if they shared the specific values espoused by the Egyptian Bloc. The fact that the alliance brought together a group of secular leaning parties with opposing economic agendas, such as the socialist Al-Tagammu Party and the pro-business Free Egyptians Party, strongly reinforced this perception.

Stances on Salient Issues

Form of Government

The Egyptian Social Democratic Party favors a mixed presidential/parliamentary form of government. According to its political platform, the party views the persistence of Mubarak-style presidentialism as "dangerous," because too much power would rest in the office of the president. However, the party believes that a pure parliamentary system could undermine national stability, due to long periods of political inactivity that commonly results from political gridlocks in such systems. Therefore, the party calls for a mixed system that would provide a stable executive leadership whose powers are limited and checked by an elected parliament.

Social Justice

The party believes that defending the social rights of all citizens is a priority and prime condition for national development. The party's stated aims include the elimination of abject poverty and narrowing the considerable income gap between Egypt's rich and poor.

The party's social program includes extending health insurance to all sectors of the population and developing unemployment benefit programs that offer training, retraining, and job placement opportunities. The party pledges to restructure subsidy programs in order to prevent wasteful spending.

Economic Policy

The Egyptian Social Democratic Party lies on the center-left of Egypt's political spectrum. It advocates social and economic justice, viewing the private sector and free market policies as the most productive and efficient way to organize the economy, albeit with a measure of state regulation.

The party further believes that the private sector should play a "leading role" in the national economy. It supports the inflow of foreign direct investment within a regulatory framework that can prevent monopolistic practices. The party's perception of the private sector highlights the importance of medium and small-sized businesses, instead of only large corporations. The platform underscores the importance of promoting investments in key industrial sectors.

The party asserts that during Mubarak's era of economic management, there was a prevalent marriage between money and political power. This marriage depleted the country's resources and is part of the reason that economic benefits failed to trickle down to the vast bulk of the country's population. The party also faults policies from the Mubarak era for the economic marginalization of the Egyptian countryside.

Religion and State

The Egyptian Social Democratic Party advocates a strictly secular state. The party's core principles state that citizenship should be based on the concept of a modern civil state, in which all citizens are treated equally with no regard to race, religion, or gender.

Military Trials and Strike Law

When the Supreme Council of the Armed Forces (SCAF) took power in February 2011, the party became a vocal opponent of trying civilian suspects in military courts. The Egyptian Social Democratic Party has also criticized laws banning strikes and sit-ins. The party has officially endorsed numerous protests against repression from authorities and in support of the right to stage labor strikes.

Foreign Relations

The Egyptian Social Democratic Party rejects what it characterizes as the Mubarak-era approach to managing foreign relations and national security. It advocates stronger Egyptian engagement with the outside world at the societal level through civil society organizations and parties.

The party's agenda focuses on issues that concern Egypt's national and regional security interests. These include water sharing conflicts with other Nile Basin countries, inter-Arab relations, and the Palestinian-Israeli conflict.

The party's documents describe Israel as a primary national security threat and calls for bolstering Egypt's military capacity for defense purposes. The party presents Palestinian national rights as one of its major foreign policy priorities.

The party opposes the abrogation of Egypt's peace treaty with Israel, preferring instead to avoid "military adventurism" that could potentially jeopardize the security of Egypt's borders. Therefore, the party calls for exerting diplomatic pressure on Israel to reach a just peace with the Palestinian people, taking steps to pressure Israel into complying with international law, and forging solid relations with Palestinians suffering under Israeli occupation.

Media Image and Controversies

The Egyptian Social Democratic Party condemned the army for violently dispersing protesters in Tahrir Square on 9 April 2011. This statement prompted Amr Hamzawy, a political analyst and later co-founder of the Egypt Freedom Party, to leave the Egyptian Social Democratic Party. Hamzawy objected to the reference to the military and claimed that the statement was adopted without his consent.

Another controversial issue surfaced in early October 2011 after party chair Abul-Ghar agreed to a highly contentious statement prepared by the SCAF, along with thirteen other parties. The document implicitly upheld the extension of Egypt's emergency law, although it offered parties some concessions related to election laws. Abul-Ghar's support of this statement was widely criticized within the party and prompted multiple resignations from dissenting members. The party later revoked its signature on the document.

During the beginning of the parliamentary election season, some party members resigned and others threatened their resignation in objection to the Egyptian Bloc electoral coalition's candidate selection process, of which the Egyptian Social Democratic Party is a member. Some party members also objected to the "undemocratic manner" through which candidates were being selected. Resignations were also made in response to allegations that some parties are fielding ex-members of the former ruling National Democratic Party (NDP) on the Egyptian Bloc's lists, much to the dismay of those who oppose ex-regime elements' participation in the elections. The Egyptian Bloc's High Commission for Electoral Coordination denied these allegations, insisting that no former NDP members made their way onto the Egyptian Bloc's lists. A Free Egyptian Party official contended that the Egyptian Bloc's list includes eight former NDP members, but insisted that none of them had been engaged in corrupt practices.

Key Figures

Farid Zahran

A founding member of the party, Farid Zahran is a publisher and civil society activist. He has taken part in a number of political initiatives, including the Egyptian People's Committee for Solidarity with the Palestinian Intifada in 2000. Zahran was also part of the Democratic Left current.

Ziad Al-Eleimi

One of the party's youngest founding members, Ziad Al-Eleimi, was part of the Social Democratic Party. This party was founded prior to the revolution but never achieved legal recognition and eventually disappeared. A lawyer by training, Al-Eleimi left the Social Democratic Party in 2009, along with a number of other members. A close associate of Mohamed ElBaradei, Al-Eleimi played a leading role in the Revolution's Youth Coalition (RYC). The RYC was a loosely affiliated group of youth-oriented opposition movements that emerged during the eighteen-day uprising that toppled former president Hosni Mubarak. It was dissolved in July 2012.

Mohamed Abul-Ghar

Mohamed Abul-Ghar, an activist and gynecology professor, founded the 9 March Movement for the Independence of Universities, which advocated for academic independence before and after the January 25 Revolution. Abul-Ghar is one of the party's most prominent personalities. He also serves as a spokesman for the National Association for Change.

Hazem Beblawi

Hazem Beblawi is a founding member of the Egyptian Social Democratic Party. He served as Egypt's deputy prime minister and finance minister in 2011 as part of the government of Essam Sharaf. Beblawi is a veteran economist and former undersecretary of the United Nation's Economic and Social Commission for Western Asia. He also served as an advisor to the Abu Dhabi-based Arab Monetary Fund. Beblawi has also led a productive academic career as a professor of economics. He taught at the American University of Cairo, Cairo University, Ain Shams University, and the Sorbonne in Paris, in addition to educational institutions in Kuwait and California.

EGYPTIAN TAHRIR PARTY

The Egyptian Tahrir Party received its official license on 5 September 2011, though party founders claim that they were in discussion about forming a party before the ouster of former president Hosni Mubarak in February 2011. Sufi leader Mohammad Alaa Al-Din Abul Azayem called on followers to join the party, purportedly in order to counterbalance the influence of rival Islamist groups such as the Muslim Brotherhood (MB) and Salafist movements.

Although the party is often described as a "Sufi" party and various Sufi movements publicly support it, the group's spokespeople are all non-Sufis. Party leader Ibrahim Zahran describes Egyptian Tahrir as a "civil party" that is open to all Egyptians and seeks greater freedom, justice, and development for all Egyptians. The party's platform, moreover, does not explicitly reflect religious leanings or agendas.

Before the Revolution

Sufi religious traditions have a long-standing presence in Egypt, with some eighty different orders active today. All these Sufi orders are members of a Supreme Council of Sufi Orders, a body that selects the "Grand Sheikh" or spiritual leader.

Under Mubarak's rule, the involvement of Sufis in political life was limited, as they were encouraged by their leaders to remain apolitical and non-confrontational toward the regime. There have been notable exceptions to this trend, however, especially in recent years. For example, during the 2010 elections Sheikh Alaa Abul Azayem, leader of the Azmiya Sufi Order, announced that he would run for parliament against Fathi Sorour, former speaker of the People's Assembly. Later, Abul Azayem withdrew his nomination and subsequently came out in support of Sorour's candidacy. He described his bid for office as an attempt to send a message to the Mubarak regime that its intervention in the religious affairs of the Sufi community was unacceptable.

Earlier in 2010, the regime intervened to resolve a power struggle within the Supreme Council of Sufi Orders. Taking the side of loyalist Sheikh Abdel Hadi al-Qasabi, then-president Hosni Mubarak appointed him as Grand Sheikh to the dismay of Abul Azayem who sought the same position. After the January 25 Revolution, some twenty Sheikhs gathered asking for the removal of al-Qasabi because of his association with the old regime.

Party Structure

Egyptian Tahrir is highly centralized. The responsibility for running the party is delegated to a party chair and a twenty-four member Executive Board, all elected by the General Assembly. The chair must receive three-fourths of the General Assembly's confidence in order to serve. The Executive Board is tasked with appointing the heads of various specialized committees, as well as local office leaders. Abul Azayem explained to *Jadaliyya/Ahram Online* that he had intentionally avoided taking any direct role in the party's leadership and appointed Secretary-General Essam Mohy Eddin in order to maintain the Tahrir Party image as an inclusive, secular organization that welcomes everyone, not only Sufis. The Elders Committee, which Abul Azayem heads, ensures that the party's policies are in line with its principles.

Parliamentary Elections

Initially, the Egyptian Tahrir Party was hesitant to participate in the parliamentary elections on grounds that big money and former ruling party figures would dominate the vote. In fact, the party threatened that it would not participate in the vote unless a law is passed to bar former ruling party figures from running in the election. Even though discussions regarding the implementation of such a law remained inconclusive until the deadline for applying for election candidacies, the party ultimately decided to participate.

The Egyptian Tahrir announced on 25 October 2011 that it would field fifty-three candidates in seven governorates, including three Copts and six women.

The Egyptian legislature is made up of 678 seats, of which 498 in the 508-member lower house and 180 in the 270-member upper house are to be elected. SCAF appointed ten members of the lower house, and ninety members of the upper house. Party officials stated that Egyptian Tahrir would only run in party-list races, but not individual candidacy races. Contrary to earlier expectations, the party did not become part of the Egyptian Bloc. Secretary General Essam Mohy Eddin said that Egyptian Tahrir views the parliamentary election primarily as an opportunity to test the party's performance, train its personnel, and participate in the new political arena.

Relationship with Other Political Parties

Attempts by the Brotherhood to pose as the leader of the entire Islamist political movement failed despite some short-lived instances of success. Tahrir Party founders have publicly denounced behaviors of Salafists alleging that followers of such movements were destroying Sufi shrines, which Salafists deem as heretical.

The Egyptian Tahrir Party has often cooperated with secular-leaning parties and has signed joint statements with them. It briefly joined the Egyptian Bloc, an electoral coalition formed by secular and liberal parties, presumably to counterbalance the influence of the Brotherhood in the 2011/2012 parliamentary elections.

Secretary General Mohy Eddin announced in late October 2011 that the party had plans to cooperate with other Sufi supported candidates, such as those affiliated with the Voice of Freedom Party.

Stances on Salient Issues

Economic Policy

The Egyptian Tahrir Party's platform advocates for a free market economy with the state interfering only to ensure social justice. The platform does not outline a detailed economic vision. Secretary General Essam Mohy Eddin explained to *Jadaliyya/Ahram Online* that the party could not establish a clear preference on these issues at such an early stage and that decisions related to economic policy would ultimately depend on the changing conditions and direction of the country.

Social Justice

While the party's platform does not explain in any detail how it plans to support social justice if elected, it identifies poverty as a major problem facing Egypt. Essam Mohy Eddin told *Jadaliyya/Ahram Online* that Egyptian Tahrir aims to support the poor and ensure decent living conditions for all. This goal, he explained, is not to eliminate social classes but rather to reduce income disparities.

Religion and State

Egyptian Tahrir supports a civil state founded upon justice and equality among all individuals. The party recognizes the importance of Article 2 of the Egyptian Constitution, which provides that Islam is the source of legislation. But the party also recognizes the rights of followers of other Abrahamic faiths to their own religious freedoms and personal status laws.

Party founder and Sufi leader, Abul Azayem, however, is often accused by other Sufi religious figures of using religion in his calls for political action. From Essam Mohy Eddin's standpoint, mixing religion and politics is nearly impossible because even Sharia is contested and has multiple branches; following all Sharia branches would be impossible. He told *Jadaliyya/Ahram Online* that the party believes that laws should not go against Sharia, but should bear its spirit. Mohy Eddin added that other parties' attempt to mix religion and politics amount to an abuse of Islam, which the Egyptian Tahrir Party rejects.

Constitution

According to Egyptian Tahrir Chair Ibrahim Zahran the party supported the adoption of supra-constitutional principles in order to ensure individual and civil rights and liberties irrespective of who is in control of the legislature.

Strikes Law and Labor Movements

Essam Mohy Eddin told *Jadaliyya/Ahram Online* that, in general, labor action is considered a healthy phenomenon. The Egyptian Tahrir Party fully supports the right to demonstrate and hold demonstrations as an integral part of the freedom of expression, but rejects actions that undermine the economy.

Media Image and Controversies

Egyptian Tahrir Party leaders are often critical when their party is labeled as the "Sufi Party" just because Abul Azayem spearheaded its creation. In September 2011, the party issued a statement claiming that while fifty percent of the party's members are Sufi, the party should not be labeled as such since it is open to all Egyptians irrespective of faith. According to Egyptian laws, parties based on religion are illegal. In the past, Sufi leaders have criticized the party's founder, Abul Azayem, for using religious rhetoric in political debates.

Given the perceived association between the Azmiya Sufi Order and the party, some observers were surprised by the decision of the Egyptian Tahrir Party not to nominate any Sufi leaders on its list of candidates, particularly Abul Azayem. While some claim that Sufi leaders are avoiding electoral candidacy out of fear that electoral defeat would shake their public image, Abul Azayem claimed that he chose not to contest in 2011/2012 parliamentary polls due to his busy travel schedule and responsibilities to followers of the Azmiya Order.

Key Figures

Ibrahim Zahran

Serving as Egyptian Tahrir Party chair, Ibrahim Zahran is an international expert on petroleum and natural gas. He is a strong opponent of Egyptian gas exports to Israel. Prior to the January 25 Revolution, Zahran was a member of the National Association for Change.

Alaa Al-Din Abul Azayem

Leader of Egypt's Sufi Azmiya Order since 1994, Mohammad Alaa al-Din Abul Azayem is one of the party's cofounders. He has often been critical of the stances of the Muslim Brotherhood and Salafist movements vis-à-vis other religious communities, including Christians and Muslim minorities. In 2010, Abul Azayem announced he would run against then-Speaker of Parliament Fathi Sorour in the 2010 parliamentary elections. Abul Azayem described his bid for office as an attempt to send a message to the regime that its intervention into the Sufi community's religious affairs was unacceptable. Abul Azayem later withdrew his nomination and supported Sorour's candidacy.

FREEDOM AND JUSTICE PARTY

The Freedom and Justice Party (FJP), the political party of the Muslim Brotherhood, could not have come into being if it were not for the January 25 Revolution. Up to that time, the Muslim Brotherhood (MB), Egypt's most powerful Islamist organization, was not only denied the right to form parties, but also barred – at lcast lcgally – from political lifc. As a rcsult, thc group had to pay a heavy price in detentions and repression to practice politics under the rule of former president Hosni Mubarak.

The group had been trying to get a foothold in the country's political arena for decades but was met with entrenched opposition by the Mubarak regime, which tended to accommodate the Brotherhood, but only within strict limits. Now, after the January 25 Revolution, the group's political ambitions have resurged on an unprecedented scale.

Freedom and Justice Party logo. Image from fjponline.com.

Officially founded in May 2011, the FJP says that it is committed to a modern state, democracy, women's rights, and national unity. The FJP's initial membership of nearly nine thousand included one thousand women and one hundred Copts. New members are subject to a probationary period of six months after which, and based on their performance record, they become eligible for permanent membership. The FJP—along with the Salafist Al-Nour Party—is one among a very few Egyptian political parties that issue probationary memberships.

The MB first thought of establishing a political party a few years ago, but the group did not actually take tangible steps toward launching it. Some MB figures, including Supreme Guide Mohammad Badie, used to oppose the idea of founding a political party, partly on the grounds that it conflicted with the group's charity work and preaching endeavors. While internal resistance toward the proposal was initially strong, it eventually receded after the revolution made the formation of a political party possible.

According to MB spokesman Walid Shalabi, the FJP and the MB share the same Islamic ideals but are separate in matters of management and finance. "Each will support the other when necessary," he said. "The MB has a bigger role than the party. As a non-governmental [institution], the MB is working on developing numerous aspects of Egyptian society, through preaching, for instance. By contrast, the FJP engages only in politics," Shalabi told *Jadaliyya/Ahram Online*. "The MB and the FJP will cooperate on certain occasions, during elections, for example," he added.

Nevertheless, observers still find it difficult to differentiate between the MB and its party, and reporters often conflate their names, partly because, in practice, the

MB and the FJP do not behave like two separate entities. For example, MB leaders gave explicit directives to their members not to join any party other than the FJP and those who chose to join other parties, such as the Egyptian Current, were reportedly expelled irrespective of their record inside the MB.

Before the Revolution

The MB was founded in 1928 by Hassan El-Banna, who was a school teacher and religious scholar. During the 1940s its influence grew very rapidly as traditional political parties, especially Al-Wafd, began to lose their credibility. On the eve of the 1952 Revolution, which deposed the monarchy, the MB was already considered the largest political group in the country. Once an ally of the Brotherhood, Egyptian leader Gamal Abdel Nasser banned political parties and eliminated the MB's political role during the 1950s and 1960s, using much violence to that end. Anwar Sadat allowed MB leaders to resume their work in the 1970s, albeit to a limited extent, and thus the MB was resurrected after an absence that lasted more than two decades. Under Mubarak, the Brotherhood was generally allowed to participate in political life without an official legal status, though the degree to which the Mubarak regime tolerated the group's activism varied over time.

The MB maintains that its foremost task is preaching and charity work, but its interest in politics has steadily grown over time.

The MB started to field candidates in the Egyptian parliamentary elections in 1984, sometimes in coalition with other parties. During the Mubarak era, it managed to score its largest electoral victory in the 2005 elections, when it won twenty percent of the seats of the legislature's lower house. It is widely believed that the former regime of Hosni Mubarak committed flagrant fraud during the 2010 election to prevent the MB from repeating its 2005 feat.

Shortly before the January 25 Revolution, the MB announced that it would not take part in the nationwide mass protests that eventually led to Mubarak's ouster—a decision that the group apparently reversed later. The group is often criticized for its initial hesitance to join the protests, even though its youth broke ranks with their leaders and participated in the 25 January demonstrations. Additionally, many MB members were quite active during the eighteen-day uprising that toppled Mubarak, and played central roles in defending the occupation of Tahrir Square by protesters, along with the rest of the political movements that took part in it.

It has remained the MB's position that the FJP is not subservient to the MB Guidance Bureau, and that would-be party leaders like Essam El-Eryan had given up their posts inside the MB before assuming the FJP's leadership. Many observers, however, believe that the Guidance Bureau's decisions and disagreements reflect on the party. In August 2011, ranking MB member Sobhi Saleh said that MB supporters would be instructed to vote for FJP candidates in the 2011/2012 legislative election. The Brotherhood, moreover, barred its members from joining any party other than the FJP, and has reportedly punished members who have not complied with that directive.

Party Structure

A Higher Council (HC) and Executive Bureau are tasked with running the party. Both bodies are elected by the General Assembly (GA), which comprises representatives from all governorates. Party members are supposed to elect their representatives in the GA for a four-year term, but the first GA members were appointed without election. The HC, also elected every four years, passes decisions by an absolute majority.

The MB's appointment of the current leaders of the FJP caused a serious rift inside the group. Many of the Brotherhood's younger members had rejected these appointments on grounds that they completely ignored the MB's youth and were made in a non-transparent manner. Dissenting youth decided to form their own party, namely the Egyptian Current. In response, MB leaders expelled these activists from the group because they violated the Guidance Bureau's orders not to join parties other than the FJP.

Parliamentary Elections

Prior to the 2011/2012 legislative election, then-FJP leader and now-president Mohamed Morsi said that, contrary to popular allegations, the MB has no intention of dominating the next parliament and wishes to see a legislature that represents all strands of Egyptian society. "We do not seek a monopoly on power, nor do we wish to control the parliament. This would not be in Egypt's best interest, which is the only thing we care for," he said. "We want a balanced parliament that is not dominated by anyone."

In what was interpreted at the time as a gesture to reassure secular forces that it would not seek to dominate national politics, the MB said in the spring of 2011 that its party would compete for no more than forty-five to fifty percent of parliamentary seats. However, as part of the Democratic Alliance electoral coalition, the FJP ended up presenting more than 500 candidates and contested more than seventy percent of the parliamentary seats that were up for election. FJP figures were at the top of over sixty percent of the alliance's forty-six electoral lists, and contested over seventy percent of individual candidacy seats. The fact that FJP eventually breached its promise not to contest more than half of the seats in parliament, and ended up securing a plurality in the lower chamber, deepened suspicions within the secular camp about the Brotherhood's intentions—suspicions that continue to animate Egyptian politics today.

During the spring of 2011, the MB, along with many political groups, embarked on a long-lasting debate over whether or not a new constitution should be put in place before elections are convened, or vice versa. A majority of the political forces argued that a constitution should be drafted first in order to clearly define the mandates of (and divisions of power between) the new parliament and president before they assume office. They also argued that the formation of the assembly that would be tasked with writing the country's new constitution should be independent of the results of the elections. The constitution, they argued, must be drafted by representatives of all walks of Egyptian political life, not the winner of one round of elections. Most of the non-Islamist political groups also needed time to get established and organized ahead of the elections.

Along with other Islamists, the MB said that a delay in elections would prolong military rule. Therefore, they pushed for convening elections as soon as possible, arguing that the concerns of their opponents could be addressed once the ruling military council transfers power to elected bodies.

Relationship with Other Political Parties

"The FJP will cooperate with all parties and political movements, not just the Islamists, as long as this is in the country's best interest," Shalabi said when asked about the FJP's relationship with other political forces.

In June 2011, the MB and seventeen other political parties, including Al-Wafd, formed the Democratic Alliance for Egypt. The alliance included more than forty political parties at one point. After a series of defections only eleven parties remained in the alliance on the eve of the 2011/2012 legislative elections, including Al-Karama and Ayman Nour's Ghad Parties. Many parties had left the Democratic Alliance due to ideological differences between Islamist and non-Islamist political forces, as well as complaints that the FJP was dominating the coalition's candidate list. The most notable defection was that of Al-Wafd Party, which was once a major partner in the Democratic Alliance. Many Wafdist figures publicly criticized their leaders' decision to forge an alliance with the MB. Some Wafdists based this criticism on the grounds that the alliance made Al-Wafd subservient to a rival organization and compromised the party's commitment to secular principles, which the MB opposes. Al-Wafd's officials, however, hold that they left the Democratic Alliance primarily because there was insufficient room on the joint candidate list for the party to field all of the candidates it had recruited.

The Egyptian Bloc, an electoral alliance founded by a group of liberal and leftist forces, was often portrayed as an attempt by secular forces to counterbalance the MB in the parliamentary elections. The fact that the alliance brought together a group of secular leaning parties with contradictory economic agendas, such as the socialist Al-Tagammu Party and the pro-business Free Egyptians Party, reinforced this perception. Some members of the bloc insisted otherwise, asserting that their alliance was not created to oppose any particular political force, stressing that Islamists were welcome to join the coalition if they shared the specific values espoused by the bloc.

The press conference launching the Egyptian Bloc's electoral campaign featured strong attacks against the Muslim Brotherhood. Al-Tagammu Party's Rifaat Al-Said accused the Brotherhood of trying to "hijack Egypt and Egyptians," and said that the group is driven by its goal to dominate politics even if it comes at the expense of national interests. Al-Said is known to be a long-standing and vehement critic of Islamist groups.

Relations between the MB and other Islamist political groups seemed tense after three Islamist parties, namely Al-Nour, Building and Development, and Al-Asala

Parties entered an electoral alliance separate from the MB-led coalition under the name the Islamist Bloc. The Brotherhood and Al-Nour eventually signed a joint document committing both sides to "clean and fair competition" in their electoral faceoff, though it is unclear why other parties were not included in the agreement.

Caught between the new Islamist parties and the secular blocs during the lead-up to the 2011/2012 elections, the FJP tried to recruit prominent independent candidates from outside the MB to run on its lists. For example, party leaders reportedly asked Hassan Nafaa to run on one of their electoral lists in Cairo. Nafaa is a prominent political scientist, public figure, and former coordinator of Mohamed ElBaradei's National Association for Change. FJP initially assured him that he would not have to officially join the party in order to run on its electoral lists. According to Nafaa, however, after accepting the FJP's offer, the party reneged on its promise and asked that he fill out a membership application in order to process the paperwork for his candidacy. Nafaa took the matter to the press, implicitly accusing the MB of opportunism.

Stances on Salient Issues

Form of Government

The FJP supports a parliamentary form of government on the grounds that such a system would provide a healthy balance between the executive, legislative, and judicial branches of government.

Social Justice

In the FJP's mission statement, "justice" is defined as consisting of three elements: (a) equality of individuals before the law; (b) social justice; and (c) solidarity among all members of society. According to the FJP's platform, social equality will only be achieved when every citizen is granted the right to participate in national production and be a recipient of state benefits. Providing basic services to the handicapped and those unable to work, the platform reads, is also imperative.

The solutions that the FJP proposes for dealing with poverty focus on encouraging public charity work and providing essential social services, as well as microloans for the poor. To reduce poverty, the FJP recommends that twenty percent of oil revenues be collected to fund welfare programs for the poor. It also recommends the restructuring of social security and subsidy systems to ensure a decent standard of living for low-income households.

Economic Policy

The FJP's platform clearly supports private ownership, private business, and free market solutions. According to the platform, the state's economic role should be limited to providing a healthy investment climate and maintaining the country's infrastructure. Hassan Malek, a businessman and ranking MB figure, said that the principles guiding economic policies followed under Mubarak were sound, but corruption and nepotism marred their implementation. He said he supported the policies that Rachid Mohamed Rachid, Mubarak's minister of trade and industries, adopted in order to boost foreign direct investments in Egypt. In contrast with Malek's remarks, the FJP's platform expresses opposition to what it describes as "the imposition of neoliberal economic policies."

The FJP also believes that the state is responsible for helping underprivileged groups by granting charity and state benefits. Additionally, the FJP contends that the state should protect workers by guaranteeing fair wages and social insurance schemes. In practice, however, party officials spoke out against labor strikes after the revolution on the grounds that they are destabilizing Egypt's already fragile economy.

The FJP is of the view that Islamic banking is beneficial to Egypt's economic wellbeing and that the country's Central Bank should promote Islamic banking modes throughout the commercial banking sector. In its platform, the FJP makes no mention of banning interest, which, some argue, is inconsistent with Islamic laws.

Gender Equality

The FJP's stance on women's rights is quite controversial. The MB itself does not allow its female members to participate in internal voting and MB officials had said that women were unfit to assume the presidency. MB leaders have once indicated that the group believes that women are entitled to run for president, but that the FJP would only support a male candidate for the position. The FJP platform does not elaborate on women's rights and the document mentions the word "women" only six times. While the FJP's position on citizenship is that all citizens are equal, the platform notes that women's rights should be subject to the principles of Sharia. In the platform's background notes, references are made to the key roles of women in education and business, as well as women's rights to defend themselves and their religion. Women also have the right to participate in public forums, to be part of decision making, and to voice their views, the FJP says in its background notes. But neither the platform nor the background notes address women's roles in leadership and top administrative posts.

Religion and State

In its platform and public statements, the FJP pledges commitment to a "civil state," which is not led by the military or clerics, but rather seeks guidance in the *makased*, or "objectives," of Sharia. Non-Muslims should be allowed to follow their own practices in matters of personal status, the FJP says. Otherwise, Sharia must offer the general frame of reference for decision-making. The platform's position on the form that the next government should take makes scant reference to religion and more or less resembles other programs of non-Islamist parties.

Minorities

The term "minorities" is mentioned only once in the FJP's platform. Still, the document advocates equality among all citizens, regardless of their religion, race, color, or gender, in all matters related to freedom of expression and the right to run for public office.

The FJP's official statements sometimes refer to Egyptian Christians and the Church as if the two are interchangeable. The platform recognizes the role of the Church in helping "Egyptians attain the goal of reform and change." The platform also reads that the Church is crucial in defending cultural values and morality, promoting political participation, maintaining goodwill between Christians and Muslims, and providing support to vulnerable groups such as orphans, individuals with special needs, and the elderly.

Military Trials

Although the FJP had been silent on the matter of military trials during the early stages of SCAF's rule, the MB Deputy Supreme Guide Mahmoud Ezzat has clearly stated that the MB opposes military trials of civilians, ending months of MB silence on the matter. Ezzat's remarks followed the trial of activist Asmaa Mahfouz.

Strike Law and Labor Movements

The FJP has not stated a clear position on a law banning strikes, which the Essam Sharaf government announced in March 2011, but Brotherhood officials have been generally supportive of the SCAF's opposition to labor strikes. FJP officials have expressed opposition to the 2011 teachers' strike on the basis that the underlying economic and social conditions are not suitable for these types of demands. Adel Hamed, assistant leader of the FJP Cairo branch, explained that the FJP was not against people demanding their rights, but rather it preferred individual demands be balanced with the greater good for society. More than once, the FJP has helped end labor strikes through mediation, as in the case of the Salheya workers. On the other hand, Muslim Brotherhood activists have attempted to force an end to teachers' strikes in some governorates in September 2011. Some reports indicate that the Brotherhood also tried to stifle the medical doctors' strike during the spring of 2011.

Foreign Relations

The FJP's platform describes the "Palestinian problem" as one of Egypt's most critical national security concerns. The party supports Palestinians' rights to form their own state with Jerusalem as its capital, as well as the right of return.

The Brotherhood's position on the Egyptian-Israeli peace treaty has been fairly ambiguous. A week after Mubarak's downfall, an MB spokesperson stated that the group respects the treaty, whereas other officials have often said it should be "revised."

Media Image and Controversies

Funding

According to MB officials, FJP funding is separate from that of the MB. The FJP says that it relies on annual subscription fees of its members, which number nine thousand. The annual fee for party membership is one hundred and fifty EGP. Some have claimed that the MB receives financial support from Saudi Arabia, but the MB has categorically denied these allegations.

Leadership

The absence of women and young people from the FJP's top ranks is worthy of note, and has been a cause for concern among young MB members. Some say that the FJP's apparent lack of interest in promoting its younger members has led some MB youths to join other parties, such as the Egyptian Current Party.

Inflexibility

The widespread impression that the MB and its party are moving toward a strict interpretation of Islamic law has prompted secular activists to denigrate the MB and the FJP. Some secular activists claim that these groups pose a threat to religious freedom, free speech, and gender equality.

Dealing with SCAF

Many activists in the non-Islamist camp alleged that the MB and SCAF struck a deal after the revolution, whereby the MB would support SCAF's policies in return for a more permissive environment for the MB to conduct its political activities. The MB and FJP repeatedly denied such allegations, but it has been noted that throughout 2011, the MB has generally refrained from participation in anti-SCAF demonstrations and sit-ins, and has often opposed them.

Key Figures

Mohamed Morsi

A former member of the MB Guidance Bureau, Mohamed Morsi served as FJP leader until summer 2012, when he was elected president. Today the party is led by longtime Muslim Brotherhood figure Saad El-Katatny. In 2000, Morsi was elected to the People's Assembly, the Egyptian parliament's lower chamber, and served as spokesperson of the MB parliamentary bloc. He lost his seat in the 2005 elections in what seemed to be a close race.

Essam Al-Eryan

The FJP deputy leader Essam Al-Eryan, a surgeon by training, is former chief of the MB Political Bureau, former member of the MB Guidance Bureau, and former MB spokesperson. Al-Eryan was arrested several times over the past three decades for political reasons. He was a member of the People's Assembly between 1987 and 1990.

Rafiq Habib

FJP deputy leader Rafiq Habib is the most prominent Copt in the party, which boasts one hundred Christians within its ranks. Critics of the FJP say that Habib's appointment is cosmetic and that his real influence does not match his senior post.

Mohammad Al-Beltagy

FJP Cairo Secretary General Mohammad Al-Beltagy, a medical doctor, was a highly visible parliamentarian between 2005 and 2010. During his tenure in the People's Assembly, al-Beltagy questioned the government's performance on major issues, including the sinking of the Al Salam ferryboat, bird and swine flu, real estate taxes, and inflation. He also played central roles in supporting the Palestinian struggle. Al-Beltagy was one of the two Egyptian Brotherhood members of parliament who were on board the flotilla, and he organized a convoy to Gaza right after Israel had released him from custody.

FREE EGYPTIANS PARTY

Prominent Coptic-Christian business tycoon Naguib Sawiris, ranked number sixty on Forbes's 2008 list of billionaires and owner of multinational enterprises throughout Africa and the Middle East, founded the Free Egyptians Party shortly after Egypt's January 25 Revolution. The party's main objective, as stated on its website, is to promote the economic and social development of Egypt, "and make it a nation in which civil rights and equality of duties prevail, free from any form of religious, gender, ethnic or social discrimination." While the party is rumored to have access to considerable financial resources due to its ties with Sawiris, it is unclear whether it will succeed in translating its allegedly vast resources to meaningful political influence.

Free Egyptians Party logo. Image from almasreyenaalahrrar.org.

The Free Egyptians Party is viewed by some observers as the most "right-wing" of the political parties to emerge in the wake of the revolution, owing to its platform, composition, and positions on various economic and social issues. When the party was established, Sawiris declared that he was expecting a conflict with well-established political groups that had been "active for eighty years"—an obvious reference to Egypt's influential Muslim Brotherhood.

In the months since the revolution, the party has expanded into a number of Egyptian governorates. With a strong and well-financed managerial and structural setup, the party, as of fall 2011, boasted some 120,000 members, including some renowned public figures such as journalist Mohamed Salmawy, poet Ahmed Fouad Negm, and young businessman Khalid Bichara. Indicators of a large Coptic majority in the party could not be confirmed, but one source indicates seventy percent.

Officially launched on 4 July 2011, the party espouses the principles of a secular civil state, with free markets and limited state involvement in economic life. Meanwhile, the party does not include social justice among its chief principles, but rather among its objectives, albeit briefly.

Before the Revolution

Sawiris never played a direct role in Egyptian politics prior to the revolution. He founded two satellite television channels in recent years, O-TV and On-TV, both of which feature political discussion and debate. At one point, On-TV featured a highly viewed talk show hosted by renowned Egyptian journalist and vocal Mubarak regime critic Ibrahim Eissa.

Sawiris's name first came to the forefront of public discussion during the 1990s when the state awarded his company Mobinil one of two mobile telephone licenses in the country. While his political leanings were not obvious at the time, it was assumed that Sawiris enjoyed good relations with the Mubarak regime, since such licenses were usually awarded to individuals with friendly ties to the ruling party. Some media reports assert that Sawiris was close to Mubarak's son, Gamal Mubarak, who was allegedly being groomed to assume the presidency after his father. After Mubarak's downfall, however, Sawiris asserted that he had differences with Mubarak's son, but acknowledged that Mubarak's rule was not entirely negative and that his own businesses and financial interests grew during the deposed president's reign.

Party Structure

The Free Egyptians' institutional structure and bylaws are unusually detailed compared to other parties. For example, the documents detailing the party's structure and bylaws are considerably larger than the party's political program. The core body of the party is its Political Office (Al-Maktab Al-Seyassy), which is elected from the party's Supreme Council, which is, in turn, elected from its General Assembly.

Party elections are conducted every four years based on simple majority. The party's bylaws state that in cases where the head of the party chooses to have two deputies, at least one must be younger than thirty-five years of age. Similarly, at least twenty five per cent of the party's Central Office members must be below the age of thirty-five.

Parliamentary Elections

The party participated in the election through the Egyptian Bloc coalition, an electoral alliance proclaiming a commitment to a strong separation between religious and political affairs. In the elections, the Egyptian Bloc fielded 412 candidates for the 508-member lower house of parliament. The bloc contested all 332 party list seats available in the lower house, in addition to fielding eighty (out of a possible 166) candidates for individual candidacy races. The legal framework that governed the 2011/2012 parliamentary elections gave SCAF the right to appoint ten of the 508 members of the lower house, and ninety of the 270 members of the upper house.

Half of the bloc's candidates were affiliated with the Free Egyptians Party, forty percent from the Egyptian Social Democratic Party, and ten percent from Al-Tagammu Party.

Relationship with Other Political Parties

The party is a member of the Egyptian Bloc electoral coalition, and participated in the 2011/2012 parliamentary elections in close coordination with its coalition partners. The Egyptian Bloc at some point included twenty-one political groups, but following successive defections during the lead-up to the election, only three parties remained in the bloc, including the Egyptian Social Democratic Party and Al-Tagammu Party, in addition to the Free Egyptians. Defections were reportedly the result of inter-party conflicts over seat shares and the relative positions of various candidates in the lists.

Disagreements were also associated with allegations that some parties were attempting to field former members of the ruling National Democratic Party (NDP) as candidates to the dismay of member groups that opposed any participation by ex-regime members in the elections. A Free Egyptian Party official conceded that the Egyptian Bloc's list included eight former NDP members, but insisted that none of them were engaged in corrupt practices.

The Egyptian Bloc was often portrayed as a "secular-leaning" alliance that sought to counterbalance the influence of the Muslim Brotherhood, specifically the Democratic Alliance's electoral coalition, which the Brotherhood's Freedom and Justice Party dominated. The fact that the bloc brought together a group of secular leaning parties with opposing economic agendas, such as the socialist Al-Tagammu Party and the pro-business Free Egyptians Party, strongly reinforced this perception.

The press conference launching the Egyptian Bloc's electoral campaign featured strong attacks against the Muslim Brotherhood. Al-Tagammu Party's Rifaat Al-Said accused the Brotherhood of trying to "hijack Egypt and Egyptians," and said that the group is driven by its goal to dominate politics even if it comes at the expense of national interests. Al-Said is known as a long-standing and vehement critic of Islamist groups.

Under the slogan "together, we will achieve what is ours," the bloc's campaign underscores goals of building a civil democratic state, and promoting economic prosperity through a liberal economy guided by a commitment to social justice. For many observers, however, it is unclear how this unlikely partnership between the Free Egyptians Party, known for its pro-business orientations, and the socialist Al-Tagammu could possibly yield a meaningful joint vision for the future of Egypt's economy. Since its inception, Al-Tagammu has sought to fight economic liberalization, as well as many aspects of the economic vision that the Free Egyptians Party espouses.

Stances on Salient Issues

Social Justice

The term "social justice" is mentioned only three times throughout the party's entire political program, although there are a handful of references to the state's responsibility for the nation's poor. The program also contains proposals to establish a minimum wage, offer unemployment benefits, and provide universal health insurance.

On the other hand, the section on education policies, while noting the importance of free education, also stresses the idea of merit-based scholarships in the provision of state support to students.

Economic Policy

While the party's program stresses free market principles throughout, there are also sections that underscore the state's responsibility for national projects, such as the Development Corridor. Proposed by Farouq Al-Baz, the Development Corridor initiative seeks to create a north-south road extending parallel to the west of the Nile, and to establish cities and agriculture land around it. The party's program also proposes fixed (i.e., non-progressive) taxes with a tax-exemption setup for low-income citizens. In 2011, Sawiris announced through his twitter account that he was preparing the party's economic program and that he was "not sure left wingers will like it," hinting to his party's commitment to fairly uninhibited free markets.

The contradiction between the party's free market-oriented vision and the economic platform of fellow Egyptian Bloc member Al-Tagammu Party is striking.

Religion and State

The party calls for the complete separation of religion and state. It proposes, however, to maintain Article 2 of Egypt's constitution—which states that Islam is the religion of the state—while guaranteeing the rights of non-Muslims to be governed by their own personal status laws.

Military Trials

As a member of the Egyptian Bloc, the party is a signatory to the bloc's statement rejecting the use of military trials against civilians. Free Egyptians Party members participated in the 9 September 2011 popular demonstration against the practice of referring civilians to military courts.

Strike Law and Labor Movements

Unlike most parties, the Free Egyptians Party quickly declared its support for the 13 July 2011 SCAF statement regarding the illegality of any behavior that would threaten the freedom of commerce during strikes and demonstrations. Although no official statement was made in relation to labor, Sawiris has expressed reservations about "sector-based" (fi'awi) strikes and demonstrations, which, he said, risk destroying the country's economic security.

Foreign Relations

The party's program supports a Palestinian state within the pre-1967 borders in accordance with international law and United Nations resolutions. It calls for enhancing economic relations with the United States outside of the confines of US assistance to Egypt.

Media Image and Controversies

Controversy surrounding the party soared in August 2011 after its cofounder Naguib Sawiris posted a link to a cartoon depicting Mickey and Minnie Mouse dressed in Islamic garb on his twitter account. Sawiris had publicly declared before that he fears Egypt could turn into a "new Iran." Sawiris, along with other party officials, has stated that he does not lead the Free Egyptians Party nor does he hold any official post inside it, though media reports continue to link them.

Party leaders' statements suggest that the Free Egyptians Party enjoys wide-based financial support. A statement by party representative Ragy Soliman to *Al-Dostour Online* declared a total budget of 6.5 million EGP, gathered from twenty-seven members, none of whom contributed more than twenty percent of the budget. A subsequent statement suggested that the funds available to the party had since increased to sixteen million EGP. The party has consistently denied allegations that Sawiris acts as the party's sole financier.

Key Figures

Naguib Sawiris

Egyptian business tycoon Naguib Sawiris joined Orascom Construction in 1979, subsequently leading the company's expansion into the field of communication technology. He established Egypt's first mobile communication network before later expanding into the telecoms market in Africa and Pakistan. During Egypt's eighteen-day uprising, Sawiris, along with other prominent Egyptian figures, was named a member of the Council of Elders, which was tasked with mediating between revolutionaries and the embattled Mubarak regime. The council did not end up playing any meaningful role.

Mohamed Salmawy

A journalist and writer, Mohamed Salmawy is the head of the Egyptian Writers' Union and former chief editor of official French-language weekly *Al-Ahram Hebdo*. He has also served as Egyptian undersecretary of state for foreign cultural relations at the Ministry of Culture.

Ahmed Fouad Negm

A celebrated Egyptian poet, Ahmed Fouad Negm is known for his fierce opposition to previous regimes, which resulted in his imprisonment on more than one occasion. The late Sheikh Imam turned Negm's poems into popular songs, many of which were chanted by revolutionaries during the eighteen-day uprising.

Khaled Bishara

Khaled Bishara is a founding member of the Free Egyptians Party. A young Egyptian entrepreneur, Bishara is group chief executive officer of Orascom Telecom Holding, one of the largest GSM operators in Egypt and Africa.

Farouk Al-Baz

A prominent Egyptian-American scientist, Farouk Al-Baz worked for NASA's Apollo Program until 1972. His proposal for a superhighway in Egypt has attracted wide attention in the wake of the revolution.

GHAD AL-THAWRA PARTY

The liberal Ghad Al-Thawra (the Revolution's Future) Party is most commonly associated with its founder, Ayman Nour, who famously ran against former president Hosni Mubarak in the 2005 presidential election. The party was originally licensed in 2004 under the name Al-Ghad Party, but it was sidelined from the political scene during Mubarak's last years in office due to internal splits and legal battles. It reemerged again as a licensed political party on 9 October 2011 under the name Ghad Al-Thawra Party (hereafter referred to as the Ghad Party).

Before the Revolution

Under the name Al-Ghad (Hizb Al-Ghad), the party made its first debut on the political scene in 2004 when it received legal recognition from the state-controlled licensing committee.

Before forming Al-Ghad, founder Ayman Nour was a prominent member of Egypt's oldest liberal party Al-Wafd, and had been one of the party's most outspoken members of parliament since he was first elected to its lower house in 1995.

As a contributor to Al-Wafd's daily newspaper during the late 1980s, a young Nour authored a set of controversial reports about police torture against detainees and suspects. These reports were at the heart of a memorable clash between Al-Wafd Party's representatives and the notorious Minister of Interior Zaki Badr in a 1987 parliamentary session. Badr charged that the photos documenting police torture of prisoners that Nour ran in Al-Wafd's newspaper were fabricated, and displayed a video clip showing what he claimed to be Ayman Nour confessing to these allegations. Badr's subsequent remarks, which featured some personal attacks against the party's leaders, prompted an attempt by Wafidst Member of Parliament Talaat Raslan to physically assault the minister of interior while he was still at the podium.

Nour left Al-Wafd Party in 2001 due to differences with then-party chief Noaman Gomaa, who four years later would face-off with Nour during the 2005 presidential election race. Other prominent Wafidsts who defected to Al-Ghad include Mona Makram Ebeid, who served as Al-Ghad's secretary-general until she left the party in 2005 in the wake of internal splits.

The legalization of Al-Ghad in 2004 raised many questions in the minds of observers, who wondered why the state-controlled Political Parties Committee would award Al-Ghad a license—the first that the state had issued in decades—unless the party was secretly cooperating with the Mubarak regime. Deepening these suspicions was the fact that this period witnessed the emergence of many "opposition" political parties that were loyal to the regime and that benefited from its largesse. These parties were pejoratively dubbed "paper parties" during the Mubarak era, in reference to the insignificance of their role.

These suspicions were quickly sidelined after Ayman Nour clashed with the state in 2005, a turbulent year for Al-Ghad Party. In January of that year the state grounded a court case against Nour for allegedly forging signatures on Al-Ghad's application for a party license. Purportedly due to US government pressure, Egyptian authorities released Nour on bail weeks later, and in September that same year he ran in Egypt's first multiparty election. During the lead-up to the vote, Nour's criticism of the incumbent president was unusually sharp at a time when personally attacking the president in public forums was the exception rather than the norm. As expected, Mubarak won the presidential poll by a landslide, while Nour picked up seven percent of the vote.

A few months after the poll, an Egyptian court convicted Nour on forgery charges and sentenced him to five years in prison, a conviction that many interpreted as the Mubarak regime's response to all the jabs that Nour took at the president throughout the election season. Egyptian authorities eventually released Nour in February 2009 on grounds that his health was deteriorating, though some assume that the decision to free the Al-Ghad Party leader was once again largely based on US pressure. Nour's case received a respectable amount of coverage in mainstream US media outlets, which viewed Nour's imprisonment as the embodiment of the Mubarak regime's defiance of Western pressures to undertake democratic reforms. It was widely reported in the media in 2008 that Nour wrote an open letter to then-US presidential candidate Barack Obama from prison, weeks before his election to office. In the letter, Nour asked Obama that Washington cease its support to Arab dictators. The document stirred controversy in Egypt as many critics accused Nour of appealing to the United States to intervene in domestic Egyptian affairs. Nour's then-wife and Al-Ghad Party leader Gamila Ismail insisted that the letter was written to Obama in his capacity as a US senator and not as a presidential candidate, and that the letter was in essence an article rather than a personal plea.

After the downfall of Mubarak in 2011, Nour had asked that the forgery case in which he was convicted be reopened, claiming that he had sufficient evidence to overturn the ruling and prove his innocence. The court, however, upheld his conviction in October 2011.

Nour's imprisonment in December 2005 was not the only blow that Al-Ghad Party had suffered that year. Also in 2005, a struggle over the party's leadership came into being with Mousa Mostafa Mousa and Ragab Hemeida on one side, and Ayman Nour and his supporters on the other. This led Al-Ghad to splinter into two factions: one headed by Mousa and another by Nour's (now former) wife Gamila Ismail. Ismail's faction held that Mousa and Hemeida were acting at the directives of Mubarak's security apparatus, which was supposedly using its allies inside Al-Ghad to purge the party from opposition elements. Mousa won a seat in the parliament's upper house in 2010, a victory that Nour described as the regime's token of appreciation to Mousa for undermining Al-Ghad Party, implying that the ruling party used illegal means to "facilitate" Mousa's victory. Similarly, Nour accused Hemeida of collaborating with the regime's security apparatus, while Hemeida countered that Nour had dealings with state security services prior to his 2005 arrest. Hemeida stood trial on charges of plotting to murder peaceful protesters during the 2011 eighteen-day uprising, or what was famously dubbed as the "battle of the camel." He was later acquitted with the rest of the defendants.

The internal split inside Al-Ghad Party persisted for years and kept it in stagnation. After a court ruled that Mousa was the party's legitimate leader in 2007, the state-controlled Political Parties Committee handed over the rights to Al-Ghad's headquarters in downtown Cairo to Mousa. This lead to a physical clash between Mousa's supporters and those of Ayman Nour and Gamila Ismail in November 2008, which ultimately resulted in the torching of the party's office. Less than a year later a court reversed that previous ruling and gave Ismail's faction control over the party's leadership; however, the Political Parties Committee refused to execute the court's directives. This ruling was annulled in July 2010 after another court recognized Mousa once again as the party's leader.

After years of political immobility due to its founder's imprisonment, legal battles, and internal strikes, the ouster of Hosni Mubarak in February 2011 was a game changer for Nour's Al-Ghad Party. Nour, who took part in the protests that eventually turned into an eighteen-day uprising that ended with Mubarak's resignation, emerged as a visible player in the Egyptian political arena. While legally Mousa is still in charge of the original Al-Ghad Party that received its license in 2004, Nour and his supporters have regrouped to form their own party, Ghad Al-Thawra (The Revolution's Future), which received an official license in October 2011.

Party Structure

In charge of running the party is a Supreme Council consisting of the party chair, the chair's deputies, and representatives from the General Assembly. The Council is elected by the General Assembly, which is the party's highest authority and is tasked with setting the party's platform and charter. The General Assembly consists of all founding party members and representatives from regional committees. Regional committees are responsible for selecting the party's nominees for parliamentary and syndicate elections.

While the party structure provides an appearance of internal party democracy, over the years Nour's rivals inside Al-Ghad have complained about what they view as his autocratic style of leadership. Former Al-Ghad secretary-general Mona Makram Ebeid was once quoted as saying: "[Ayman Nour]...does everything. He's the head of the party. He's editor-in-chief [of party paper Al-Ghad]. He's a member of parliament. He's the head of the board. He doesn't listen to anyone."

Parliamentary Elections

In the parliamentary elections, Al-Ghad Party fielded fifteen candidates (thirteen for the lower house and two for the upper) through the Democratic Alliance for Egypt, a Muslim Brotherhood dominated electoral coalition. The Brotherhood's Freedom and Justice Party (FJP), which fielded over five hundred candidates, topped over sixty percent of the alliance's forty-six electoral lists, and contested over seventy percent of individual candidacy seats. Al-Ghad Party's candidates were mostly concentrated in Nile Delta governorates, with the exception of two candidates in Assiut, and one in Sohag. There were 688 parliamentary seats in total up for election (498 in the lower house and 190 in the upper house). The legal framework that governed the 2011/2012 parliamentary elections gave SCAF the right to appoint ten of the 508 members of the lower house, and ninety of the 270 members of the upper house.

Prominent Al-Ghad figure Gamila Ismail did not run through the Democratic Alliance's candidate rosters, but rather as an independent candidate. She contested an individual candidacy race in the Cairo district of Qasr Al-Nil, but lost.

Relationship with Other Political Parties

Al-Ghad Party is a member of the Democratic Alliance for Egypt, along with ten other political parties, most notably the Muslim Brotherhood's FJP, the nationalist Al-Karama, and the Islamist-leaning Labor Party. The alliance once brought together over forty political parties but witnessed mass defections due to what many groups described as the FJP's control over decision making and dominance over the coalition's joint candidate rosters. The continued participation of Al-Ghad in the Democratic Alliance was significant, because it was one of the few liberal parties inside the coalition with some name recognition. Many believe that the Muslim Brotherhood was keen on keeping small, non-Islamist parties inside its coalition in order to portray its electoral bid as the product of a broad national consensus rather than an attempt to single-handedly dominate the electoral field.

Observers had expected that Al-Ghad would follow the thirty-some parties that defected from the coalition in early October 2011 after realizing that the Brotherhood would leave little room on the electoral rosters for fellow members of the coalition. Al-Ghad remained, nevertheless, deciding to settle for only two percent of all the parliamentary seats available for election. Ayman Nour justified the decision to stick with the alliance despite his party's negligible share in its candidate rosters by saying that Al-Ghad chose to look beyond seat shares in order to help build national consensus around a single electoral list. Given the Brotherhood's domineering role in the alliance and the withdrawal of most of its politically significant members, many observers were unconvinced that the coalition truly reflected the wide "national consensus" it professed to represent.

Media Image and Controversies

Since its founding, Al-Ghad Party has struggled in presenting itself as more than just "Ayman Nour's party." The party's efforts to prove itself a significant political force with a meaningful following took a huge blow in 2011 after its decision to contest only a handful of seats in the 2011/2012 parliamentary elections. The party's limited participation in the elections reinforced the perception that Al-Ghad has a negligible following and is little more than Ayman Nour's political arm.

Stances on Salient Issues

Form of Government

Al-Ghad Party calls for a parliamentary system with well-defined limits on presidential authority. It further believes in decentralized government.

Social Justice

Al-Ghad Party professes a commitment to social justice without heavy-handed state intervention. It advocates the implementation of a progressive tax system and tax exemption for low-income households. The party calls for unemployment benefits and supports the right to free education for all citizens. Its platform states that social security programs should be managed through agencies that are monitored but not run by the state.

Economic Policy

The party supports only limited state intervention in the economy for the purposes of protecting private property, supporting public education and healthcare, and protecting against monopolistic practices. Al-Ghad pledges to promote foreign investments and small and medium enterprises. It calls for lifting laws criminalizing financial bankruptcy. The party's platform calls for dismantling the ministries of justice and information, and for the privatization of state-owned media outlets.

Religion and State

The party's official platform does not offer a detailed vision for the role of religion in public life, though it calls for lifting all forms of religious discrimination in state policy.

Party leader Ayman Nour expressed support for Article 2 of the constitution, which designates Islam as the main source of legislation, but said he rejects calls for establishing an "Islamic state."

Military Trials

The party condemns the practice of referring civilians to military courts. It has been reported that Ayman Nour's son, Nour Nour, is an active member of the "No to Military Trials" campaign.

Al-Ghad pledges to reform the ministry of interior and place it under civilian leadership.

Strike Law and Labor Movements

The party supports workers' right to strike and stood in opposition to the 2011 law banning that practice. Al-Ghad Party was one of the participants in the 30 September 2011 Tahrir Square demonstration dubbed "Reclaiming the Revolution," which called for ending this law.

Foreign Relations

Al-Ghad is not in favor of abrogating Egypt's peace treaty with Israel, but party leader Nour said that he does not rule out the possibility of amending the accord in order for Egyptian forces to gain full sovereignty over Sinai, including the right to deploy its forces in the peninsula. He has said he supports Palestinians' right to a state. Nour welcomes relations with the United States as long as they do not compromise the independence of Egyptian decision-making.

Nour's relationship with Washington has been the subject of close public scrutiny due to US government efforts to pressure Egyptian authorities to release Nour from prison between 2005 and 2009. Rivals have criticized Nour for being "too close" to the United States.

Key Figures

Ayman Nour

Ayman Nour is the Ghad Party chair. Born in the city of Mansoura in 1964, Nour began his political career in Al-Wafd Party, where he started out as a journalist in the party's daily newspaper in 1984. He served as director of the party's Center for Political and Strategic Studies from 1990 to 1995. He was first elected to the parliament's lower house in 1995 and was re-elected in 2000. Due to disagreements with then-Wafdist leader Noaman Gomaa, he left the party and went on to form Al-Ghad Party in 2005. Nour is most known for his unsuccessful presidential bid in 2005 against then-incumbent Hosni Mubarak. Nour was sentenced to five years in prison in 2005 on charges of fraud, and was released in February 2009, presumably due to US government pressure. His imprisonment was largely seen as politically motivated due to his vocal criticism of the Mubarak regime. In October 2011, a court decision upheld his 2005 conviction after Nour's request for a retrial.

Al-Karama Party

Supporting an Arab nationalist agenda, Al-Karama (Dignity) Party has been part of the Egyptian political landscape since 1997, when its founder, Hamdeen Sabahi, broke ranks with the Nasserist Party. Al-Karama believes that Egypt represents the fountainhead of Arab nationalism, and a true Arab renaissance can only be realized through social equality and scientific and cultural development. While the party was "founded" more than a decade before the January 25 Revolution, it only received legal status in August 2011.

Before the Revolution

Party founder Sabahi ran in the parliament's lower house elections for the first time in 1995 as an independent candidate, even though he was a member of the Nasserist Party at the time. He ran again as an independent in the 2000 and 2005 elections, because Al-Karama Party never managed to obtain a formal party license under the Mubarak regime.

Sabahi was the first member of parliament to publicly raise the issue of Egyptian gas exports to Israel. In line with his party, Sabahi maintained a firm stance against the construction of a separation barrier along Egypt's border with the besieged Gaza Strip.

In 1997, Sabahi was arrested and charged with inciting agricultural workers to stage an open-ended sit-in on their land in protest against a new law regulating the relationship between landowners and tenant farmers. The new law effectively reversed land reforms implemented in the immediate wake of the 1952 revolution. The raft of new reforms allowed landowners to impose enormous rent increases and evict tenant farmers.

Al-Karama Party logo. Image from gomhuria-online.com

Al-Karama's activists were among the founders and leaders of the Kefaya movement. Kefaya emerged in 2004 as the first protest movement demanding that Hosni Mubarak resign as president and refrain from passing the presidency onto his politically influential son, Gamal Mubarak. The party was also active in the National Association for Change. This coalition of opposition figures and groups formed in 2010 to demand democratic reforms and free and fair presidential elections in which independent candidates that were not handpicked by the Mubarak regime could run.

Party Structure

A Supreme Authority is tasked with running the party, executing the General Assembly's decisions, appointing heads of the party's media organizations and its unelected board members, and forming shadow governments. The General Assembly, which is responsible for formulating the party's platform and its policies, elects members to the Supreme Authority and the party's leader. Local party units, prevalent throughout Egypt in local districts, villages, and cities are tasked with electing members of the General Assembly. The party has an Executive Bureau comprised of high-ranking leaders. Al-Karama also has a Political Bureau that includes the party's leader, along with co-founders Amin Iskandar, Kamal Abu Eita, and Abdel Rahman Al-Gohary.

Parliamentary Elections

Al-Karama Party fielded sixteen candidates in the parliamentary polls. Ten of these candidates ran on the electoral lists of the Muslim Brotherhood-led Democratic Alliance for the 508-member parliamentary lower house and three ran for the 270-member upper house. The remaining three contested individual candidacy seats. The Muslim Brotherhood's political party, Freedom and Justice, dominated the Democratic Alliance's candidate rosters. The legal framework that governed the elections gave SCAF the right to appoint ten of the 508 members of the lower house, and ninety of the 270 members of the upper house.

Al-Karama contemplated leaving the Democratic Alliance because of a conflict with the Freedom and Justice Party over the relative positions of its candidates on the electoral lists. However, Al-Karama ultimately decided to contest elections through the Democratic Alliance.

Party leader Amin Iskandar justified the decision to join the Islamist-led alliance by saying that the Al-Karama Party opposed electoral divisions between liberal and Islamist forces. He stressed, however, that his party's program was independent and distinct from other parties on the list.

Another party leader, Saad Aboud, who is also contesting parliamentary polls, said that Al-Karama's place on the Democratic Alliance's list could allow the party to capture as many as eleven seats in parliament.

Sabahi had pledged that he would not contest the presidency as Al-Karama's nominee, and ended up running as an independent candidate in 2012. After Al-Karama was licensed in August 2011, Mohamed Sami became the party's official leader.

Relationship with Other Political Parties

Although Al-Karama has considered abandoning the Democratic Alliance, it ultimately decided to stay on and field its candidates in the parliamentary elections through the coalition's electoral lists. Al-Wasat Party leader Abul Ela Maadi claims that Al-Karama, as well as other parties, turned down his proposal to form a "third-way" electoral coalition separate from the political forces that are divided across Islamist-secular lines.

Al-Karama's presence in the Democratic Alliance was significant, nonetheless, as it was one of the few parties with a noteworthy political history that remained in the coalition. This helped temper a common perception that the alliance was but a "one-man-show" run by the Muslim Brotherhood (MB). Some believe that the MB was keen on keeping smaller, non-Islamist parties in a coalition alongside its own party, Freedom and Justice, in order to present its electoral gains as the product of a broad national consensus that extends beyond pro-Islamist political communities. The Democratic Alliance, which was once comprised of over forty parties, entered the elections with only eleven. Many parties had left the Democratic Alliance in the lead-up to elections, alleging that the Freedom and Justice Party was dominating the alliance's decisions and its electoral lists, a suspicion that was later confirmed when the alliance submitted its final lists.

As a Nasserist political party with political and ideological differences with the MB, Al-Karama's continued partnership with the MB is perplexing to some observers. Some claim that Al-Karama's activists have played a role in stifling the Muslim Brotherhood's entry into the Kefaya movement between 2005 and 2006. In May 2010, Amin Iskandar expressed reservations concerning Mohamed ElBaradei's comment that the Muslim Brotherhood should be allowed to govern Egypt. Iskandar stated that the Islamist group has yet to offer clear positions on critical issues, such as citizenship and women's rights.

Stances on Salient Issues

Form of Government

The party favors a system of government that limits presidential authority and grants the prime minister complete power as a representative of the executive authority. The party also supports a system of government that allows parliament to draft and approve laws and monitor government performance.

Social Justice

The party seeks a profound, albeit equitable, redistribution of wealth and resources in Egyptian society, along with poverty alleviation measures through state planning and social welfare programs.

Economic Policy

According to Al-Karama official Saad Aboud, the party seeks to establish a social democratic system and reclaim the government's central role in state planning.

Religion and State

The party believes that religion represents an essential cultural component of Egyptian society but does not support a theocratic system of governance. The party does, however, take a firm stance against secularism. Al-Karama's program states that secularists "want to separate nationalists from their past and present and insert them into a contemporary western scene totally alien to them."

Military Trials

Al-Karama's Youth Secretary Hossam Moanis Saad told *Jadaliyya/Ahram Online* that the party opposes the practice of referring civilians to military courts. Party officials have repeatedly called for restricting the use of such trials to military personnel who are charged with crimes that were committed during the Mubarak era.

Strike Law and Labor Movements

The party rejected the March 2011 law banning labor strikes. Al-Karama stresses the importance of respecting workers' constitutional right to strike, which the party holds should not be revoked or criminalized.

Foreign Relations

The party opposes normalization of relations with Israel and says that it wishes to see the peace treaty between Egypt and Israel annulled. When *Jadaliyya/Ahram Online* asked about the possibility of unilateral action in this regard, Al-Karama's Youth Secretary Moanis said that such a decision would be left up to the Egyptian people, who should be given a chance to vote on the issue in a national referendum.

Media Image and Controversies

In 2006, Al-Karama Party was under severe attack from many political activists after its official newspaper ran a front-page feature on the achievements of the then-Libyan leader Muammar Al-Qaddafi under the title "Thirty-Seven Years of Achievement." This led some activists to accuse Al-Karama of receiving financial support from the former Libyan regime, while others questioned Al-Karama's democratic commitments. Some critics of the party have questioned how a group could demand an end to Mubarak's twenty-five years of rule, while simultaneously singing the praises of Qaddafi, who ruled Libya with an iron fist for thirty-seven years. Shortly after the outbreak of the rebellion against Qaddafi, which ultimately led to his demise, Al-Karama leader Sabahi said that he "supports the Libyan people against the tyrant Qaddafi."

The ambiguity surrounding Al-Karama's position on the 19 March 2011 constitutional referendum was also perplexing. Before the referendum was approved by seventy-seven percent of Egyptian voters, the SCAF-proposed constitutional amendments unleashed heated, often hostile, debates throughout the country. Liberal and leftist activists opposed these amendments on the grounds that they failed to overhaul the "authoritarian constitution" inherited from the Mubarak era, whereas Islamist groups claimed that approving these amendments was the best way to ensure a swift end to military rule. While most parties took clear positions on these amendments, Al-Karama remained silent for much of the lead-up to the vote. Party leader Hamdeen Sabahi avoided taking clear positions until media outlets began reporting that Al-Karama supported the amendments, forcing Sabahi to side unequivocally with the "No" camp that opposed them.

Key Figures

Hamdeen Sabahi

A graduate of Cairo University's mass communications faculty, Hamdeen Sabahi founded Al-Karama Party in 1996 after defecting from the Nasserist Party due to disagreements with its leader, Diaeddin Daoud. Under Mubarak's rule, Sabahi repeatedly tried to obtain official party status for Al-Karama by applying to the state-controlled Political Parties Committee and filing cases with the Political Parties Court. His efforts in this regard were to no avail.

Sabahi was elected to the lower house of parliament in 2005 and initially expressed interest in running in the 2005 presidential election, but later called upon citizens and opposition groups to boycott the poll. He is a founding member of the National Association for Change reform movement, formed in early 2010.

Sabahi initially ran in the 2010 parliamentary elections, but withdrew his candidacy after he allegedly witnessed vote rigging by Mubarak's ruling party.

Sabahi participated in the January 25 Revolution from the outset, and was slightly injured while protesting in Kafr Al-Sheikh in the Nile Delta. In 2012, he ran in the presidential election race, but was eliminated after the first round of voting.

Amin Iskandar

Veteran political activist Amin Iskandar is a founding member of Al-Karama Party and a longstanding advocate of Nasserist pan-Arabism.

Iskandar participated in the 1977 bread riots in Cairo. Beginning in 1978, he was arrested several times for his political activism.

In the 1980s, he helped organize the campaign to defend Suleiman Khater, an Egyptian soldier who was accused of opening fire against Israeli tourists in Sinai. Iskandar also served as the coordinator of a popular campaign against normalization with Israel. Additionally, Iskandar was a founding member of the Kefaya protest movement.

Prior to Al-Karama Party's launch, Iskandar's political activities included establishing the Socialist Forum with Kamal Al-Din Refaat, the Socialist Party with Farid Abdel-Karim, the Alliance Party with Kamal Ahmed, and the Nasserist Party with Diaeddin Daoud.

Kamal Abu Eita

Kamal Abu Eita is a founding member of Al-Karama Party. A student of philosophy, psychology, and law, Abu Eita's prominence grew when he succeeded in founding an independent union for Real Estate Tax Collectors in 2009. As Egypt's first independent workers' syndicate established during the Mubarak era, the union started a trend that has gathered more force since the January 25 Revolution.

Abu Eita is the general manager of the Real Estate Tax Collecting Directorate in Giza, secretary-general of the Committee to Defend Political Prisoners, and founder of the National Committee to Defend the Rights of Workers and Agricultural Workers.

After the revolution, Abu Eita reportedly turned down then-Deputy Prime Minister Yehia Al-Gamal's offer to serve as Egypt's minister of manpower and emigration.

Abu Eita submitted an application to run in the parliamentary polls with Al-Karama Party on the Democratic Alliance's list. However, his application was refused by the state-run Elections Commission on the grounds that the committee does not recognize the Egyptian Federation of Independent Labor Unions, of which Abu Eita is president. According to Abu Eita, the committee's decision directly contradicts the post-revolution Constitutional Declaration, which guarantees workers the right to establish independent unions. A court ruling later reversed the Elections Commission's decision on 16 November 2011.

National Progressive Unionist (Al-Tagammu) Party

Together with the Nasserist and Al-Wafd Parties, the National Progressive Unionist Party (NPUP), commonly known as Al-Tagammu, was considered one of the main three opposition parties in the pre-revolution era. It initially emerged in 1975 as a socialist platform in the Arab Socialist Union (ASU), Egypt's only party at that time.

Following President Anwar Sadat's decision to transform Egypt's one party system into a limited multi-party one, Al-Tagammu withdrew from the ASU to form its own party in April 1976. At the time, Sadat had envisioned organizing politics via three platforms that existed inside the ASU: rightwing (the Liberal Socialist Organization, Al-Ahrar Al-Eshtarakyeen); center (Egypt Arab Socialist Organization, Tanzim Masr Al-Araby Al-Eshtraky); and left (the National Progressive Unionist Organization, which later became Al-Tagammu Party). Sadat eventually repackaged the ruling party into the National Democratic Party (NDP).

Al-Tagammu was thus established to occupy the Left Forum (minbar) of Sadat's new semi-pluralist system. Khaled Mohieddin—a former member of the Free Officers Movement which started the 1952 Revolution—led the initiative to form Al-Tagammu together with a number of prominent socialist figures, including Mahmoud Amin Al-Allam, Lotfy Al-Kholy, Fouad Morsi, Hussein Abdel-Razek, Amina Shafiq, Shahinda Maqlad, Ismail Sabry Abdullah, and many others.

While most of the party's influential founding members came from Marxist backgrounds, the party was designed from the start as a platform for "the left" at large and hence emerged with significant membership from the non-Marxist left including, Nasserists, trade unionists, and syndicalists. Thus, the platform of the party was designed in broad enough terms to accommodate diverse trends inside the organization. Although this uneasy balance proved difficult to manage at some points, it persisted until the 1990s when the Nasserists finally left Al-Tagammu to form their own party, leaving behind a more homogenous socialist party.

The 1980s is commonly viewed as Al-Tagammu's golden age, when it was still able to attract many supporters from the left. During the mid-1980s the party was able to boast as many as 150,000 members including an active core of 20,000 members. It also managed an official weekly paper that circulated as many as 130,000 copies (*Al-Ahaly*). The party's growth came to a halt in the late 1980s, however. By the late 1990s it was already starting to shrink, losing influence and entering one crisis after another. Now it is largely a stagnating party managing a party paper with a limited number of readers.

The 1990s were marked by the collapse of the Soviet Union and the subsequent loss of faith in socialism. The Nasserist Party was formed in this period, taking away a significant part of Al-Tagammu's membership and spheres of influence with it. At the time, Al-Tagammu also played a leading role in supporting the state's crackdown on Islamists, effectively siding with the Mubarak regime on this matter. Rifaat Al-Said, the party's current chair, previously stated that his view of Mubarak's rule "depends on the changing political conditions and the way the government treats us. We cannot deal with Mubarak in the same way we used to deal with Sadat. Sadat suppressed us fiercely. But as this is no longer the case; we have to change too."

Before the Revolution

In the past, Al-Tagammu opposed the regime quite forcefully on several fronts. It led, for instance, a fierce battle against Sadat for signing a peace treaty with Israel. This earned it Sadat's fury and led to the detention of its leadership among other prominent figures during the infamous 1981 arrests of political dissidents. The party also played an important role in hosting and promoting actions in solidarity with the Lebanese resistance in 1982, the two Palestinian intifadas, and opposing the 2003 Iraq war during Mubarak's reign. With respect to economic issues, Al-Tagammu was always firm in opposing the economic liberalization programs of both Mubarak and Sadat and was equally committed to supporting labor and agricultural workers' rights and struggles.

In acting on these issues the party always adopted and promoted peaceful democratic means of change. As such, it participated in all parliamentary lower house elections that took place since the formation of the assembly in 1979. Between 1976 and 1990, the party held no parliamentary seats but still enjoyed some electoral influence. During the 1976 elections, for example, the party originally won three seats but Sadat dissolved this parliament in response to mounting opposition against him in 1979. Al-Tagammu failed to win any seats in the 1979 round that came to replace the dissolved parliament.

In 1984, elections were carried out via proportional representation for the first time in Egyptian history. Al-Tagammu won 4.8 percent of the national vote, falling 3.2 percent short of the minimum needed to enter parliament. The same scenario was repeated in 1987 when the NPUP won only 2.8 percent of the total votes, again failing to translate the votes it received into seats.

Al-Tagammu participated in the 1990 elections, thereby breaking an opposition-wide boycott that came in response to the regime's elimination of judicial monitoring of the poll. As a result, Al-Tagammu's reputation was tarnished, with the party depicted as having sabotaged the opposition's boycott plans. The party won five seats (roughly one percent of the parliament's lower house) making it the largest opposition bloc in parliament. Al-Tagammu held these five seats, more or less, in each of the elections that followed (Khaled Mohieddin in Kafr Shokr, Qalubiya; Loufty Waken in Kafr Sakr, Sharqiya; Mohamed Abd Al-Aziz Shaaban in the Cairo district of Hadaiyek Al-Koba; Al-Badry Farghali in Port Said; and Mokhtar Gomaa in Kom Ombo, Aswan). In the 2005 elections, however, the party won only two seats.

Al-Tagammu contested elections for the upper house (Shura Council) as well, usually without managing to win any seats. The one seat it maintained in the upper house was the one it gained via presidential appointment from Mubarak. Like most opposition parties, it never turned down this appointment.

A few days before the beginning of the January 25 Revolution, Al-Tagammu leader Rifaat Al-Said said he opposed the protests scheduled for 25 January on grounds that they were poised to ruin "National Police Day." After demonstrations began gaining momentum, Al-Said later announced that Al-Tagammu Party activists could not participate in the demonstrations because they were in detention. He also added that the party would have agreed to participate in the protests if it were not for the fact that they were organized on a day that was meant to celebrate and honor police officers. The protests, which were in part a backlash against police brutality, ultimately turned into a mass uprising, which led to the ouster of former president Hosni Mubarak.

Party Structure

The party is organized along several central and regional divisions. The central divisions are the main decision making sectors of the party. They include, the General Conference, the Central Committee, the General Secretariat, the Political Bureau, and the Central Secretariat.

Al-Tagammu has one of the most extensive organizational structures and developed internal procedures among Egyptian parties. Many of those who have defected from the party, however, claimed that in practice all powers remain in the hands of the chairperson.

Technically speaking, the General Conference is the party's highest authority, responsible for setting and amending its charter. It is composed of delegates from the governorates' committees, members of the Central Committee, and representatives of the Progressive Youth Union and the Progressive Women Union.

The Central Committee is responsible, in turn, for translating the directives of the General Conference into concrete management tasks, policies, and plans, in addition to electing one or more deputy chairperson, the general secretary, and the assistants of the general secretary. The committee consists of the presidency of the General Conference (about five to ten members), about one hundred members elected by the General Conference, the secretaries of the governorates, and representatives of the party's youth and women's unions. The size of the Central Committee can vary and expand up to twenty percent of the General Conference.

The Political Bureau is the entity that oversees the development of political positions on various matters and the formation of policies and strategies. It is composed of the chairperson of the party, who is elected by the General Conference, and a number of members elected by the Central Committee. On the other hand, the general secretary is a member of both the Political Bureau and the Central Committee. He/she heads the General Secretariat, which is composed of the deputy chairpersons, the general secretary, and his or her deputies, in addition to the secretaries of the governorates and the party's MPs. The General Secretariat is responsible for managing the party's political and administrative staff and coordinating work between the different organizational levels of the party. Friction has often existed between the general secretary, the Political Bureau, and the chairperson, who is the most powerful figure in the party.

Parliamentary Elections

Al-Tagammu participated in the 2011/2012 parliamentary elections as part of the Egyptian Bloc. The Egyptian Bloc fielded 412 candidates for parliamentary lower house elections. The bloc contested all 332 party list seats available in the 508-member lower house, in addition to fielding eighty (out of a possible 166) candidates for individual candidacy races. The legal framework that governed the elections gave the Supreme Council of the Armed Forces the right to appoint ten of the 508 members of the lower house.

Al-Tagammu occupies only ten percent of the bloc's joint lists, while the Free Egyptians Party and Social Democratic Party occupy fifty percent and forty percent respectively.

According to Hussein Abdel-Razek, the chief of Al-Tagammu's Political Bureau, the party did not have a real chance of winning a large number of seats because its candidates were placed at the tails of the Egyptian Bloc's lists. Only two of Al-Tagammu's candidates are featured in high positions on the bloc's lists, in Aswan and Sharqiya. In addition to party list candidates, Al-Tagammu nominated fifteen candidates for individual candidacy seats, but they faced difficulties because of their limited campaign budgets, Abdel-Razek said. The party used to enjoy a number of electoral strongholds: in Cairo's Hadaiyek Al-Koba, one consistent seat in Alexandria, and another in Aswan and North Sinai. The party, however, lost popularity in many of these areas due to resignations and defections.

Relationship with Other Political Parties

Historically, Al-Tagammu Party used to vehemently refuse cooperating with the Muslim Brotherhood, or for that matter Islamists at large. Al-Tagammu allegedly did so on principle and this led it to tacitly condone measures that the Mubarak regime employed to reduce the Muslim Brotherhood's electoral gains. Some believe, for example, that the regime rigged certain races in the 2010 elections in favor of Al-Tagammu candidates in order to undermine Muslim Brotherhood candidates. Al-Tagammu's relationship with the Muslim Brotherhood is therefore rife with tensions, and the same goes for its relationship with the Brotherhood's FJP.

Despite Al-Tagammu's historical tensions with the Muslim Brotherhood, the party showed significant pragmatism in its decision to contest the elections via the Democratic Alliance, an electoral coalition dominated by the Muslim Brotherhood's FJP. Al-Tagammu announced it would exit the coalition in the wake of a controversy: that activists affiliated with Islamist members of the alliance instigated strife at the demonstrations held on 29 July 2011 under the banner "The Friday of Unity and Popular Will." The Friday demonstrations were initially aimed at emphasizing national unity and, among other things, the need to cease military trials of civilians. Al-Tagammu alleged that Islamist activists failed to adhere to the demonstrations' formal demands—which were agreed to in advance—and instead decided to promote divisive slogans calling for the establishment of an "Islamic state" and the implementation of Sharia law. The Islamist organizations responsible for propagating these slogans on 29 July denied having agreed to any set of collective demands prior to the demonstration.

Al-Tagammu participated in the parliamentary elections as part of the Egyptian Bloc, an electoral alliance founded by a group of liberal and leftist forces that was often portrayed as a secular coalition trying to counterbalance the Muslim Brotherhood. The fact that the alliance brought together a group of secular leaning parties with contradictory economic agendas, such as the socialist Al-Tagammu and the pro-business Free Egyptians Party, reinforced this perception.

The press conference launching the Egyptian Bloc's electoral campaign featured strong attacks against the Muslim Brotherhood. Al-Tagammu Party's Rifaat Al-Said accused the Brotherhood of trying to "hijack Egypt and Egyptians" and said that the group is driven by its goal to dominate politics even if it comes at the expense of national interests.

Again, Al-Tagammu showed considerable pragmatism in accepting to enter the Egyptian Bloc, a coalition dominated by what is perceived to be Egypt's most pro-business party: the Free Egyptians Party. For many, the fact that Al-Tagammu would accept such a small share (ten percent of the Bloc's seats) in its partnership with a group espousing principles it opposed throughout its history explains the extent of its decline.

The party has already lost most of its most important members, including many of those who stayed with it during its years of glory and decline, such as Abdel Ghaffar Shukr and Abul Ezz Al-Hariri, both of whom left Al-Tagammu to form the Socialist Popular Alliance Party (SPA). Al-Tagammu's relationship with the SPA is therefore also troubled.

Stances on Salient Issues

Form of Government

Before the January 25 Revolution, Al-Tagammu used to support a parliamentary form of government that reduces the omnipotent authorities given to the president under the 1971 Constitution. After the revolution, many secular parties began to favor a strong presidential system. They feared that a weak president would lead to the Muslim Brotherhood dominating the executive via a strong presence in parliament. It is unclear if Al-Tagammu has shifted its position, as the issue is not discussed in the party's media and its leaders tend to give inconsistent answers on this issue.

Social Justice and Economic Policy

The party always stood against the economic prescriptions of the IMF and the World Bank, accusing them of increasing poverty and the gap between the rich and the poor. Al-Tagammu also opposes the privatization of the public sector, and has engaged in popular mobilization to protect whatever is left of it. Al-Tagammu also calls for a fairer distribution of national income and the return of privatized factories to the public sector.

The relevance of these positions in Al-Tagammu's electoral campaigns was limited, since it participated in the 2011/2012 elections through the Egyptian Bloc electoral coalition, which advanced some positions that seem to contradict Al-Tagammu's own platform. Under the slogan "together, we will achieve what is ours," the bloc's campaign underscored the goal of promoting economic prosperity through a liberal economy committed to social justice. For many observers, it is unclear how this unlikely partnership between the Free Egyptians Party, known for its pro-business orientations, and the socialist Al-Tagammu could possibly yield a meaningful joint vision for the future of Egypt's economy. Since its inception, Al-Tagammu has sought to fight economic liberalization, as well as many aspects of the economic vision that the Free Egyptians espouses.

Military Trials

The party unequivocally opposes subjecting civilians to military tribunals and Al-Tagammu members participated in many protests and rallies that spoke against this practice.

Foreign Relations

The party opposes "US imperialism" and the normalization of Egyptian-Israeli relations. Historically, the party has consistently opposed the Camp David Accords. Al-Tagammu professes support to Palestinians' right to self-determination, and played a significant role in opposing the Israeli occupation of Lebanon in 1982 and US-led wars on Iraq.

Media Image and Controversies

The party has been suffering internal conflicts ever since its formation. Early conflicts generally centered on competition between Al-Tagammu's Marxists and Nasserists over the party's leadership. This episode ended with the defection of the Nasserists who subsequently formed their own party.

More recent conflicts revolved around internal opposition to the party's current chair, Al-Said, who was often accused of striking deals with the Mubarak regime. Such conflicts escalated in the aftermath of the 2010 elections, when many of the party's members demanded Al-Tagammu's withdrawal from what was viewed as one of Egypt's most farcical elections. Al-Said refused to withdraw, and the regime allegedly ended up rigging some races in favor of Al-Tagammu candidates. In response, some Al-Tagammu activists froze their memberships. Others tried to formally withdraw confidence in the party's chair but failed to amass enough power to successfully do so.

The party experienced a wave of resignations right after the January 25 Revolution, all in protest of Al-Said's autocratic-style in managing the party. On 13 March 2011 seventy-three Central Committee members froze their membership and pledged not to return until Al-Said is replaced. Headed by long-time Al-Said opponents Abul Ezz Al-Hariri and Abdel Ghaffar Shukr, this group eventually left the party to form the Socialist Popular Alliance Party with other leftist activists.

Another attempt to withdraw confidence in Al-Said took place on 12 October 2011, and although the majority of Central Committee members voted against Al-Tagammu's leader, the number of participants at the meeting did not pass quorum.

Key Figures

Rifaat Al-Said

Born in 1932, Rifaat Al-Said is a founding member of Al-Tagammu Party and its current chair. He is also one of its most controversial figures. His political history goes back to the mid-twentieth century when he was a member of the Communist Party dismantled by the late President Gamal Abdel Nasser. Al-Said was detained during the 1958 wave of arrests of communists and served four years in prison.

In addition to his involvement in politics, Al-Said is also an academic. He holds two doctoral degrees in modern history. He is also a part-time lecturer at the American University in Cairo. He has written several books that focus mostly on Islamists and the communist movement, including *Pages from the History of the Muslim Brotherhood*, *History of the Socialist Movement in Egypt*, *Egyptian Socialist Organisations*, and *History of the Communist Movement in Egypt*.

Al-Said is known as a diehard enemy of the Islamists. He was typically accused of striking under-the-table deals with the former regime out of opposition to the Islamists and in return for seats in parliament. He fought vehemently to get his party to participate in the infamous 2010 elections against the will of many party activists. These elections were viewed as the most rigged in Egyptian history, and some analysts attribute the 2011 uprising—at least in part—to this event. Many political parties boycotted those elections, but Al-Tagammu refused to join the opposition boycott under pressure from its chair. Al-Said was appointed to the upper house of parliament by Mubarak in the aftermath of the 2010 elections, an appointment he did not turn down.

Said almost lost a vote of confidence because of the party's participation in the second round of the 2010 elections, surviving it at considerable symbolic loss. On 13 October 2011, he announced his resignation from the party under mounting pressure for his ouster. The resignation was not finalized since the General Secretariat rejected it.

Hussein Abdel-Razek

Born in 1936, Hussein Abdel-Razek is a founding member of Al-Tagammu, its secretary general, and a member of its Political Bureau. Abdel-Razek is currently considered the party's second man and one of the main candidates for leading it after Rifaat Al-Said. Although both figures have been closely allied in many internal battles, Abdel-Razek is now one of Al-Said's main adversaries.

Abdel-Razek used to write frequently in Al-Tagammu's weekly *Al-Ahaly* and has authored several books dealing with various aspects of Egyptian political life.

Nabil Zaki

Nabil Zaki is the spokesman of Al-Tagammu and a potential candidate for chairing the party after Al-Said. He graduated from the Department of Philosophy at Cairo University in 1955. A journalist by profession, Zaki is a respected public speaker. He now leads the "reform and renewal movement" of Al-Tagammu, fighting against Al-Said's well-entrenched allies.

Amina Shafiq

Amina Shafiq is a well-known journalist and political activist. She was among the intellectuals arrested in the notorious wave of arrests in 1981, when Sadat ordered the detention of most of Egypt's activists, politicians, and intellectuals. In the aftermath of the fraud-ridden 2010 elections, then-president Mubarak appointed her a member of parliament—one of ten the president can appoint to the lower house under the constitution. Shafiq did not decline this appointment despite the wave of public anger that followed the 2010 parliamentary elections.

AL-NOUR PARTY

Established in the wake of the 25 January uprising, Al-Nour (The Light) Party is the largest of Egypt's three licensed Salafist parties (the other two being Al-Asala and Al-Fadila parties). It was established by Al-Da'wa Al-Salafiyya (The Salafist Call), Egypt's largest Salafist group, commonly known as Al Da'wa Movement. Al-Da'wa started in Alexandria, where it now enjoys a considerable following.

Al-Nour Party was officially licensed in June 2011. Official registration is of paramount importance in Egypt at the present time, as the current election law limits the right to contest two-thirds of the seats of the parliament to a limited number of officially registered parties, including Al-Nour. Under the rule of former president Hosni Mubarak, the state generally did not allow for the formation of Islamist parties, but after the revolution many Islamist groups managed to obtain official political party license.

Before the Revolution

Even though Salafists seemed uninterested in forming parties before the revolution, Yasser Borhami, a prominent Salafist preacher and a leading figure within Al-Da'wa, called for the establishment of a political party that would work to unify Egypt's Islamic movement and apply Islamic principles to all aspects of social and political life.

Many of Al-Nour's current members had been involved in Al-Da'wa, which has a presence all over Egypt and boasts a particularly formidable stronghold in Alexandria. Prior to the ouster of former president Hosni Mubarak, the group had not been closely engaged in opposition politics on the grounds that it was considered sinful to oppose a Muslim ruler. Salafist leaders even discouraged their followers from participating in the 25 January demonstrations, which ultimately turned into a mass popular uprising. Al-Nour Party spokesperson Nader Bakar once stated that the Salafists' refusal to demonstrate on 25 January had been a positive step, because, otherwise, "the Americans would have ordered Mubarak to massacre them all."

Al-Da'wa activists, however, participated in forming popular committees, which helped maintain security in neighborhoods throughout the country after the nationwide withdrawal of police forces on 28 January 2011. After the ouster of former president Mubarak, Al-Da'wa began to directly compete for political power in the country.

Party Structure

The Supreme Council, responsible for running the party, consists of thirty to forty members, all elected by the General Assembly, which itself includes between 150 to 200 representatives and founding party members from each governorate. The supreme council is tasked with electing the party chair and secretary-general, along with party secretaries for political affairs, administrative affairs, and media affairs.

The Supreme Council also elects members of the party's Governing and Regulation Committee.

The party offers two types of membership, "affiliated membership" and "working membership." All individuals who join the party are considered "affiliated" members until they complete an orientation about the party and its principles, after which they become "working" members. Al-Nour is one of the very few parties in Egypt that employ a probationary membership system. Another party that issues a probationary membership system is the Freedom and Justice Party of the Muslim Brotherhood (MB).

Parliamentary Elections

Al-Nour Party contested the 2011/2012 parliamentary elections through the Islamist Bloc (officially dubbed the Alliance for Egypt), which brought together Al-Asala Party and the Building and Development Party, the latter having been formed by the once-militant Islamic Group (Al-Gamaa Al-Islamiyya).

Al-Nour contested close to ninety percent of parliamentary seats in the 2011/2012 election. Al-Asala's candidates were largely concentrated in Cairo, while the Building and Development Party fielded candidates in Upper Egypt on behalf of the Islamist Bloc.

Al-Asala had unveiled plans to cede to Al-Nour all of the seats in the governorate of Alexandria, where Al-Nour's mother organization, Al-Da'wa, has historically enjoyed significant influence. Salafist groups also reportedly enjoy considerable influence in the northern governorate of Kafr Al-Sheikh, presumably because many of their younger cadres complete their higher education in the Salafist stronghold of Alexandria. Salafist influence is also said to be strong in the Upper Egyptian governorate of Assiut and the Imbaba district of Giza (Greater Cairo), a notorious stronghold of radical Islamist organizations that often witnessed violent clashes between Islamists and the security forces of the former regime.

Al-Nour Party logo. Image from alnourparty.org

The Islamist Bloc had anticipated stiff competition in Upper Egyptian governorates from affiliates of Mubarak's now-defunct National Democratic Party (NDP) and its offshoots, particularly those hailing from powerful and well-connected Upper Egyptian families. Thus, Al-Nour unveiled plans to launch voter awareness campaigns and mount legal challenges against those candidates once tied to the former regime.

The Islamist Bloc fielded 693 candidates in the parliamentary polls. On its part, Al-Nour contributed 610 candidates to the coalition's electoral rosters, which included 477 candidates for the parliament's lower house, and 133 candidates for the upper house. Al-Asala and Building and Development competed for only forty and forty-five seats, respectively, leaving more than eighty-five percent of the joint candidate roster to Al-Nour. Earlier in the parliamentary election season, Al-Nour Party's spokesperson once refused to specify the proportion of seats contested by each of the three parties of the coalition on the grounds that Al-Nour did not want to belittle the role of its two coalition partners. The legal framework that governed the elections gave SCAF the right to appoint ten of the 508 members of the lower house, and ninety of the 270 members of the upper house.

The coalition competed for seats in all of Egypt's governorates, except for Sinai. The regime of former president Hosni Mubarak had previously prevented Salafist movements from operating in that region. While the Islamist Bloc's electoral lists for the election included women, none of its candidates were Copts. Al-Nour once stated that it is willing to consider fielding Coptic candidates, as long as those candidates represent the party's platform. Party officials claim that a handful of Copts had been among Al-Nour's founding members.

The party's announcement that it would field sixty female candidates in the elections became the source of considerable controversy, since many Salafists do not believe that women should vote, let alone run for office. In response, Al-Nour leader Emad Abd Al-Ghafour stressed that the party was committed to the principle that men and women should not mingle, and that the decision to field female candidates had been a necessary measure aimed at winning as many seats as possible, given that the law stipulates a set quota for female candidates on party lists. Al-Ghafour went on to note, however, that female candidates would remain at the tail end of the list and would therefore have very little chance of securing representation.

The Islamist Bloc announced plans to wage its electoral campaign under the slogan, "Together, we will build Egypt: A modern identity and state built with Egyptian hands and minds." Al-Nour had pledged to refrain from using religious slogans, or from campaigning inside mosques, in the lead-up to the parliamentary polls, although one party official was quoted as telling supporters that voting for Al-Nour candidates represented a form of almsgiving that would someday be rewarded in heaven.

During the 2011 Eid holiday, moreover, Al-Nour activists competed with those of the MB's Freedom and Justice Party over control of public prayer venues and spaces, as both parties sought to keep their names in the spotlight in religious forums convened during the Muslim holiday.

Prior to the elections, spokesperson Bakkar said that the Islamist Bloc would rely on an international marketing company to design its campaign ads, stressing that none of the candidates affiliated with the coalition would spend more than the legally mandated campaign-spending cap of 500,000 EGP.

Relationship with Other Political Parties

Al-Nour had been part of the Muslim Brotherhood (MB)-led electoral coalition, the Democratic Alliance, before it defected in September 2011. According to reports,

Al-Nour withdrew from the coalition due to disagreements with the MB's political party, Freedom and Justice (FJP), over its share in the coalition's joint candidate lists.

Party spokesperson Bakkar said in a press conference that Al-Nour's dispute had not been with the FJP, but rather with liberal and secular parties.

Prior to the vote, the Muslim Brotherhood and Al-Nour signed a joint document committing both sides to "clean and fair competition" in their electoral faceoff, though it is unclear why other parties were not included in the agreement. Nevertheless, the two Islamist coalitions competed fiercely over votes cast by Islamist constituents who previously had little choice but to vote for the MB.

Stances on Salient Issues

Form of Government

According to Bakkar, the party supports a hybrid form of government combining elements of a presidential political system with that of a parliamentary one, along the lines of the current French system.

Social Justice

The party's platform states that there should be a "just and equal distribution" of income and wealth among the Egyptian public. This contrasts with most mainstream parties, which usually call for establishing a decent minimum wage without explicit reference to the need for wealth redistribution. Al-Nour's platform invokes the Islamic concept of "zakat," which stipulates that well-to-do Muslims should allocate fixed portions of their annual incomes to the poor.

Economic Policy

According to the party's platform, the national economy should be managed in conformity with Islamic principles, which should also inform legislation governing the banking sector and loan finance. The party rejects loan interest on grounds that it contradicts Islamic values. The platform also underscores the importance of anti-trust laws and the government's role in protecting consumers against monopolistic practices, both were subjects of heated debates in Egypt before the January 25 Revolution.

Al-Nour further calls for promoting national agricultural production so as to allow Egypt to attain a degree of self-sufficiency and food security, an area where the country is considered particularly vulnerable. The party is also committed to raising the budget designated for research and development in the civil and military industrial fields to at least four percent of Egypt's gross domestic product.

Religion and State

Al-Nour spokesperson Bakkar said that Al-Nour's campaign motto and its emphasis on "identity" reflect the raison d'être of the Islamist Bloc's parliamentary bid, namely "the application of Sharia (Islamic Law) in a gradual way that suits the nature of society." Bakkar's statement implicitly refers to a common belief among many Islamist activists that Egypt's journey to the complete application of Sharia should be slow and gradual so as not to alienate people. The term "modern state," Bakkar added, signified neither a secular state based on conventional Western understandings nor a fundamentalist religious state, but rather a modern state that relies on science in pursuing progress and prosperity.

Yasser Borhami, considered a godfather of the party, once wrote that Islam was "both religion and state" and could not be separated from politics, although he stressed this was not an endorsement of a theocratic state. Like many Al-Nour officials, Borhami emphasizes the importance of Article 2 of the Egyptian Constitution, which holds that Islam is the religion of the state. Al-Nour's leaders often criticize the use of terms like "civil" or "secular" state, arguing that secularism does not mean the separation of religion and politics, but rather the complete alienation of religion from life altogether. Secularism, they argue, amounts to atheism.

Prominent party members, however, have not always adhered to the pragmatism reflected in the aforementioned positions. For example, Hazem Shouman, a well-known Salafist cleric who ran in the elections on Al-Nour's list, told a gathering in Mansoura on 6 November 2011 that Islamic and Islamist rule is imminent and there is nothing that secularists can do to stop it. Shortly after this statement, Shouman crashed the stage of a concert by singer Hisham Abbass in Mansoura University, and told attendees that such concerts were sinful.

Military Trials

The party completely rejects the practice of trying civilian suspects in military courts, describing it as a serious threat to Egyptian political life.

Strike Law and Labor Movements

The party states that the worker's right to strike is lawful, while also being guaranteed by international conventions. Al-Nour offsets this assertion, however, by adding that strikes are "undesirable" at the present time, since they could adversely affect the economy during Egypt's critical transitional phase.

Foreign Relations

The section on foreign relations in Al-Nour's political platform is atypically brief, outlining a broad commitment to enhancing Egypt's regional and international role and improving its relations with neighboring countries. There is no mention of the party's stance vis-à-vis Palestinian rights or the Egyptian-Israeli peace treaty, although the document stresses the importance of respecting existing treaties and conventions.

Al-Nour Party once indicated that it opposes the annulment of the Egyptian-Israeli peace treaty, but called for revising some of its provisions. In another instance, however, it pledged to decide on the future of the treaty through a national referendum.

Media Image and Controversies

Al-Nour's quick emergence in the political arena after the January 25 Revolution has raised many questions in the minds of observers of Egyptian politics. Many wonder how a movement like Al-Da'wa—typically perceived as an apolitical movement that was tolerated by the Mubarak regime to pacify political Islamist trends—was quickly able to form a political party with sufficient resources to contest and campaign for almost all the seats in parliament. This has led speculators and political rivals to accuse Al-Nour of receiving foreign funding from like-minded governments like that of Saudi Arabia and Qatar. Officials of the ministry of justice have confirmed that Salafist organizations received grants worth hundreds of millions of pounds from Qatari organizations after the revolution.

While it has not publicly disclosed its sources of funding, Al-Nour officials have denied these claims, and its spokesperson challenged that anybody could present evidence proving that the party receives foreign funding. Saudi officials have also denied these allegations.

Nevertheless, assertions that Al-Nour receives external funds kept circulating in the lead-up to the 2011/2012 parliamentary elections, especially as the party's relative extravagance came to the fore. In one case, Al-Nour, together with Al-Da'wa, were able to transport about two million people to Cairo from all over Egypt to participate in the 29 July 2011 Tahrir Square demonstration, which was considered the largest Islamist public gathering in Egyptian history. Al-Nour also managed to erect a grand platform in Tahrir Square that overshadowed the platforms of all other parties, including the more established MB. Speculation as to where the party received its funds intensified, particularly that Al-Nour's constituency is believed to be largely drawn from the rural poor, and to a lesser extent the urban poor.

External funding of political groups remains a thorny issue in Egyptian political debates. It is usually raised in relation to entities that accept funding from US-based institutions. While concerns have been raised about possible Saudi and Qatari funding of Islamist groups, US funding remains the more sensational topic in the Egyptian media.

In early October 2012, Al-Nour's youth activists spoke out against a decision by party leader Emad Abd Al-Ghafour to sign a statement committing the signatories —which included figures from various political parties—to a set of SCAF-proposed political reforms. The statement, dissenters within the party complained, lent SCAF unconditional support, did not address the ongoing application of Egypt's hated emergency law, and failed to provide a timetable for the swift transition from military to civilian rule.

The party's decision to field female candidates in the elections was reportedly a source of contention within Salafist circles. While the party holds that female participation in politics—as both voters and legislators—is religiously unacceptable, it has tried to repair its image vis-à-vis women's rights by convening a gathering of its female activists. The party's detractors, however, cynically mocked this initiative, pointing out that none of the speakers at the event were women, but rather a handful of old men lecturing female attendees about the nature and scope of their political rights. While Al-Nour's platform states that men and women are equal with respect to human dignity, it underscores "the importance of maintaining differences in their human and social roles."

Al-Nour was criticized for refusing to include photos of its female candidates alongside those of its male nominees in its electoral flyers, simply inserting the image of a flower above the names of women running on the party's lists.

Key Figures

Yasser Borhami

A co-founder of Al-Nour Party, Yasser Borhami is one of Egypt's most prominent Salafist clerics and vice president of Al-Da'wa Movement. While he does not have an official post inside the party, Borhami—as vice-chair of Al-Da'wa, Al-Nour's mother organization—appears to hold considerable influence over party decision-making. Observers consider Borhami a particularly controversial figure due to his relatively strict religious opinions.

In July 2011, Borhami supported a SCAF-issued statement calling for a halt to public demonstrations so as to avoid chaos and instability. Notably, Borhami discouraged Al-Da'wa supporters from taking part in the 25 January protests, which ultimately culminated in Mubarak's ouster. A few weeks earlier he was criticized for his attempts to calm down public uproar over the death of Salafist activist Sayed Belal in the custody of State Security Investigations Services in early January 2011. Belal, who was arrested in connection with a church bombing in Alexandria in December 2010, was reportedly tortured to death while in police custody. While non-Islamist groups like the April 6 Movement blamed Egyptian authorities for Belal's death and called for punishing those responsible, Borhami, to the disappointment of disgruntled Salafist activists, asked followers to "be patient" and exercise restraint.

Born in Alexandria in 1958, Borhami graduated from Alexandria University with a degree in medicine, after which he studied Islamic Law at Egypt's prestigious Al-Azhar University.

Hazem Shouman

A Salafist cleric closely associated with the party, Hazem Shouman ran on the Islamic Bloc's list in the city of Mansoura. He is commonly known as the cleric who attacked presidential hopeful Mohamed ElBaradei by questioning his commitment to Islam, although he later apologized for the remarks.

Shouman is well known outside Islamist circles for his widely cited quote in which he stated, "A civil state means your mother cannot wear the hijab." Shouman told a gathering in Mansoura on 6 November 2011 that Islamic and Islamist rule is imminent and there is nothing that secularists can do to stop it.

Reform and Development Party - Misruna

The Reform and Development Party (RDP) was established in 2009 by Mohamed Anwar Esmat Al-Sadat (commonly known as Esmat Al-Sadat), a nephew of late Egyptian president Anwar Sadat. Egyptian authorities turned down RDP's initial license application in July 2010, but the party was eventually legalized in May 2011 in the wake of Egypt's January 25 Revolution.

In June 2011, the RDP merged with Misruna (Our Egypt), a party founded by business tycoon Ramy Lakah who was pushed out of the liberal Al-Wafd Party in April 2011. The nascent party therefore now refers to itself as the Reform and Development-Misruna Party (RDP-M). The RDP-M defines itself as a civil party calling for comprehensive economic and political reform and promoting sustainable development.

Al-Sadat currently serves as the RDP-M's chair although Lakah was initially poised to serve as the party's first chair. The political party's licensing committee had objected to Lakah's appointment on legal grounds, namely that he was not one of the RDP's founding members when it was first licensed.

Before the Revolution

The RDP had limited experience in political activism prior to the eighteen-day uprising that led to the ouster of President Hosni Mubarak. The party took part in a February 2009 popular campaign opposed to Egyptian gas exports to Israel. In the 2010 parliamentary polls, the RDP fielded some candidates, including Al-Sadat himself. Like many candidates affiliated with parties and groups that lacked legal status at the time, RDP candidates officially ran as "independents."

Al-Sadat was elected to parliament on an independent ticket in 2005. He was a critic of Mubarak-era practices and policies, including the alleged grooming of presidential scion Gamal Mubarak to succeed his father, the decades-old emergency law, and the country's unpopular privatization drive. In 2006, Al-Sadat submitted a motion in parliament calling for investigating longtime Mubarak aide and member of parliament Zakaria Azmi for corruption allegations. Shortly thereafter, the Mubarak regime retaliated against Al-Sadat. Ruling party allies in the legislature succeeded in suspending Al-Sadat's parliamentary membership in May 2007 on the legal grounds that he lost the integrity to hold that office in accordance with article ninety-six of the constitution after a court ruling declared him bankrupt. Another court, however, reversed that ruling in September 2007. A year earlier Al-Sadat's late brother, Talaat, had also entered into a showdown with the regime. He was accused of defaming the Egyptian army after suggesting that the military was complicit in the assassination of his late uncle president Anwar Sadat. After his parliamentary membership was similarly suspended, a military court sentenced Talaat to a year in prison in October 2006.

RDP-M leader and famous French-Egyptian businessman Ramy Lakah also had a brief experience in politics during the Mubarak era. An influential figure among

Egypt's small Roman Catholic community (less than one percent of the population), Lakah is said to have played a role in organizing Pope John Paul II's visit to Egypt. In 2000, he was elected to parliament as the representative of Cairo's Azbakeya district, but a 2001 court order suspended his membership on grounds that he held dual citizenship. Lakah fled Egypt in 2003 due to mounting debts, though he claims that the government made it difficult for him to reach a fair settlement with his creditors in order to force him out of parliament after he beat an influential National Democratic Party (NDP) figure in the 2000 elections. Years later, Lakah reached a debt settlement deal and returned to Egypt in March 2010. Following his return, he reportedly said he would support a Hosni Mubarak bid for another term as president.

Party Structure

A Supreme Council is in charge of managing the party's affairs. It is supported by a judicial authority known as the Council of Elders and an executive authority tasked with implementing the directives of the Supreme Council. The RDP-M's interim bylaws provide for the election of party leaders.

The official party line appears to reflect Al-Sadat's stated positions on various issues. Lakah's engagement in the party's affairs remains unclear.

Parliamentary Elections

The RDP-M announced its support of at least two hundred candidates in the 2011/2012 lower house parliamentary polls. The party has presented candidates in all of Egypt's governorates except the Red Sea. Its candidate rosters include RDP-M leader Esmat Al-Sadat who won an individual-candidacy seat in the governorate of Menoufia.

Relationship with Other Political Parties

The party did not participate in any electoral coalition, though there had been some talk of limited coordination efforts with other liberal parties in individual candidacy races.

Stances on Salient Issues

Form of Government

The RDP-M advocates for a mixed system of government that combines elements of presidential and parliamentary systems. In such a system, the platform explains, the president would appoint a prime minister who would then appoint the cabinet. The president must in turn approve the prime minister's cabinet appointments.

Economic Policy

According to its official platform, the party supports economic freedom and espouses free-market policies. It stresses the importance of private sector participation in development, direct investment, and trade. In its program, the party attempts to distance itself from "predatory capitalism" by endorsing a supervisory and regulatory role for the state.

Social Justice

The platform contains a detailed national development plan that aims to improve living standards in economically marginalized governorates, especially in rural Upper Egypt and the Sinai Peninsula. It also called for improving Egypt's national education system and enhancing Egyptian industry, agriculture, and small businesses. The party's political program stresses the importance of advancing the rights of women and minorities.

Religion and State

RDP-M calls for a civil state in which all citizens enjoy the freedom of belief. It opposes the establishment of political parties based on religion. Al-Sadat has repeatedly called on liberal political forces to offset Egypt's influential Islamist current.

Strike Law and Labor Movements

While the party supported demands by laborers and professionals to organize independent unions under the Mubarak regime, it has adopted a more cautious approach to the issue of labor strikes after the January 25 Revolution. In 2011, the RDP-M kept its distance from Egypt's burgeoning protest scene in order to focus on the elections and, as party officials have said, "not waste time in political debates."

Military Trials

The RDP-M has not released an official statement on military trials for civilians and there is no record of its official participation in demonstrations organized in protest of that practice. In a statement dated 9 May 2011, Al-Sadat urged SCAF to refer those responsible for attacking Egyptian churches to military trials.

Al-Sadat has expressed support for SCAF, stating that Egypt's military is the only institution capable of guaranteeing the security of the state. He has repeatedly called on Egyptians to support SCAF until the executive authority can be delegated to an elected civil government.

Foreign Affairs

RDP-M's platform offers only brief discussion of foreign policy. Al-Sadat has called for maintaining a relationship built on equality with the United States and Israel and has defended Egypt's peace treaty with Israel. He has called the continued demilitarization of Egypt's Sinai Peninsula a necessity, but has also said that the treaty should be amended in the future if needed.

Media Image and Controversies

Some observers label RDP-M as an offshoot of the former ruling NDP, presumably because of its founder's association with late president Anwar Sadat's family. While RDP-M chair Anwar Esmat Al-Sadat has never contested elections on an NDP ticket, some reports claimed that that his party's candidate rosters included individuals who were once affiliated with the NDP. Al-Sadat maintains that his party has not fielded any former NDP elements in the 2011/2012 elections.

Key Figures

Mohamed Anwar Esmat Al-Sadat

Party founder Mohamed Anwar Esmat Al-Sadat was an outspoken critic of the Mubarak regime. He was especially critical of Mubarak's influential son, Gamal Mubarak, and steel magnate and regime stalwart Ahmed Ezz. Many observers believe that his criticism of the former regime cost him his parliamentary membership in 2007, when he was abruptly suspended from parliament on the ground that a court declared him bankrupt—although another court later reversed that ruling.

Al-Sadat, who has served on Parliament's Foreign Relations and Economic Committees, has long been a controversial figure, having been accused of corruption in 1983 following the death of his illustrious uncle.

Ramy Lakah

A French-Egyptian multi-millionaire, Ramy Lakah is chairman of the Lakah Group, an industrial and healthcare conglomerate. He was elected to parliament in 2000, but fled the country shortly afterward to escape his mounting debts, thought to have reached as much as two billion EGP. A few months later, his parliamentary membership was annulled as a result of his dual citizenship.

After settling his finances with creditor banks, Lakah's case was dropped and he returned to Egypt in March 2010, after which he ran for parliament as an Al-Wafd Party candidate (claiming to have relinquished his French citizenship). After his Al-Wafd Party membership was suspended, he formed the Misruna Party, which subsequently joined forces with the RDP to become RDP-Misruna.

SOCIALIST POPULAR ALLIANCE PARTY

The Socialist Popular Alliance Party (SPA)—founded immediately following the ouster of former president Hosni Mubarak—was the first Egyptian leftist party to be legally recognized after the January 25 Revolution. On 28 September 2011, the party was officially registered, having met the quota of 5,000 signatures needed for licensing.

Before the Revolution

The SPA had no presence before the revolution but it brings together a number of leftist groups, which were active prior to the revolution, including the Socialist Renewal Current, Democratic Left, and Al-Tagammu Party. Activists associated with the 1970s student movement have also joined SPA's ranks.

The SPA has attracted many of the Al-Tagammu members who left their party after Egypt's 2010 elections to protest the party's participation in what were clearly fraudulent elections. They have been joined by members of the Socialist Renewal Movement. The latter is a splinter group of the Revolutionary Socialists, which was created in 1995 by Trotskyite student groups. Another group that joined the SPA includes members of the Democratic Left, an organization that was established in 2007 and modeled after Europe's social democratic parties.

After the January 25 Revolution, the Revolutionary Socialists quickly split up and the majority of its members founded the Egyptian Social Democratic Party, while a minority joined the new Democratic Workers' Party and SPA.

SPA's main objective is to serve as a unifying platform for the Egyptian left, which is the function that Al-Tagammu used to serve. Before the 2011 revolution, Al-Tagammu was viewed as the left's uniting front and had been able to rally together leftists of all leanings.

A thorn in the side of former president Anwar Sadat during its early years, Al-Tagammu adopted a more conciliatory tone toward the regime during the 1980s, thereby risking its credibility as the voice of the Egyptian left. Some say that Al-Tagammu was co-opted by the Mubarak regime, as evidenced by its strong opposition to Islamist groups like the Muslim Brotherhood.

The SPA has not, however, been able to co-opt all leftist platforms in the country. Leftist parties that were formed after the ouster of Mubarak, including the Democratic Workers' Party and the Egyptian Socialist Party, remain outside the SPA. Older leftist groups, including the Egyptian Communist Party, have also refrained from joining SPA.

Party Structure

The SPA has a Constituent Assembly and a Secretariat. Assembly members are elected by local committees from various governorates, as well as function-based committees (e.g., student and media committees). The SPA Assembly elects the Secretariat, which includes at least one member from each local and function-based committee.

Parliamentary Elections

The SPA initially planned to participate in the elections through common lists with the Egyptian Bloc, an electoral alliance founded by a group of liberal and leftist forces. However, SPA chose to leave the Egyptian Bloc, allegedly because other participating parties allowed former ruling National Democratic Party members to run on the bloc's lists.

The SPA decided instead to run on shared lists with the Revolution's Youth Coalition, Egyptian Current Party, Egypt Freedom Party, Equality and Development Party, and Egyptian Alliance Party. The lists of these parties are called Al-Thawra Mostamerra (The Revolution Continues). According to its members, the Revolution Continues Alliance (RCA) comprised an ideologically diverse set of actors, namely liberal, Islamists, and socialists, including the youth of the Muslim Brotherhood who defected from the group and helped form the Egyptian Current Party.

Through 280 candidates (out of a possible 332), the RCA contested thirty-four (out of a possible forty-six) party list races for the 508-member lower house of parliament. Additionally, twenty-six (out of a possible 166) candidates contested individual candidacy races. The legal framework that governed the elections gave the Supreme Council of the Armed Forces the right to appoint ten of the 508 members of the lower house.

According to Egyptian Current Party leader and former Muslim Brotherhood member Islam Lotfy 100 of these candidates were below the age of forty. The majority of candidates that the alliance fielded belonged to the SPA, according to RCA member Khaled Abdel Hamid. Some thirty-two were affiliated with the Egyptian Current Party.

Titled "Security, Freedom, and Social Justice," the RCA's platform, which it announced in November 2011, focused on re-establishing law and order, promoting social justice, and closing the income gap between the rich and the poor. It also called for securing a swift transfer of power from the ruling military council to an elected civilian authority by mid-2012.

Relationship with Other Political Parties

The SPA was previously part of the Egyptian Bloc electoral coalition, which also included the Free Egyptians Party, Egyptian Social Democratic Party, Egypt Freedom Party, Al-Tagammu, Egyptian Communist Party, Democratic Front Party, Awareness Party, Sufi Tahrir Party, and Socialist Party of Egypt. The alliance was formed by several liberal, social democratic, and leftist groups, and was commonly viewed as an attempt to counterbalance Islamist trends in the legislative elections. However, the Socialist Popular Alliance, among others, left the Egyptian Bloc when other parties in the coalition allegedly began accepting former NDP members into their ranks. The only parties that ultimately remained in the bloc were the Free Egyptians Party, Al-Tagammu, and the Egyptian Social Democratic Party.

The decision to join the Egyptian Bloc was already the subject of controversy within the SPA, as many members objected to joining a coalition that is primarily counter-Islamist in its orientation and that includes pro-business parties such as the Free Egyptians Party. The majority of the party's members, however, supported the decision to join the Egyptian Bloc initially when it was created on 15 August 2011. The decision to withdraw came less than two months later.

The SPA ultimately decided to field its candidates through RCA electoral coalition. The RYC and the Egyptian Current Party almost withdrew from the RCA one week before the candidate registration deadline, objecting that the SPA was dominating the top positions of all lists at the expense of the youth groups. The problem was quickly renegotiated to allow more youth members to be placed in prominent positions on party lists.

Stances on Salient Issues

Social Justice

The SPA supports a minimum wage in addition to a maximum wage that does not exceed fifteen times the minimum wage. It took part in demonstrations calling for the minimum wage to match the 2010 court-mandated level of 1,200 EGP per month.

Economic Policy

The SPA is committed to a social welfare state with free healthcare and education, as well as state support for cultural and artistic activities. Its economic program advocates for ending privatization initiatives launched under the Mubarak regime. It also seeks to ensure previous privatization deals are audited to ascertain the presence or absence of corruption.

The SPA further calls for restructuring Egypt's social insurance and pension program. Social security programs, the party maintains, must be managed by the National Organization for Social Security and supervised by program beneficiaries.

Religion and the State

The party supports a civil democratic state and its members are mostly proponents of the separation of religion and state.

Minorities

The SPA program also upholds a constitution that does not discriminate between its citizens on grounds of religion, beliefs, gender, or race. Some party members helped create the nonprofit Egyptians Against Religious Discrimination.

Military Trials

The SPA is firmly against military trials of civilians. The party has participated in numerous activities protesting this practice and signed several statements condemning the use of military tribunals.

Strikes and Labor Movements

The party is a strong supporter of labor movements and workers' right to strike. The party and its members have supported labor movements and demands for better working conditions and more just wages.

Foreign Relations

On foreign relations, the SPA is for ending the Qualified Industrial Zone agreement with Israel and for terminating the exportation of Egyptian gas and cement to that country. It also urges the severing of all trade and economic relations with Israel.

Media Image and Controversies

According to SPA member Gihan Shabaan, conflicts inside the party in the lead-up to the 2011/2012 elections centered on how to relate to Islamist groups and pro-business liberal parties. Members were split between those who wished to enter into an alliance with pro-business liberal parties, such as the Free Egyptians Party, and those who argued that alliances should be based on social and economic considerations only rather than one's position on the Islamist/non-Islamist divide.

Key Figures

Emad Ateyya

Emad Ateyya was a leftist student activist during the 1970s and a member of one of the underground organizations that eventually formed the Egyptian Communist Party. He left the Egyptian Communist Party in 1987 to help create the People's Party (Hezb Al-Shaab).

Ateyya was one of the organizers of the Egyptian Popular Committee in

Solidarity with the Intifada, an Egyptian movement created in solidarity with the second Palestinian Intifada.

Atteya also played a major role in the Engineers against Guardianship, a movement advocating the lifting of court-ordered custodianship of Egypt's Engineers' Syndicate. Judicial guardianship was imposed on the syndicate in 1995 on grounds that the syndicate's General Assembly had committed financial violations. Engineers against Guardianship, in which Ateyya was an active member, argued that this order was part of a regime-sponsored scheme to restrict dissent and political freedoms.

Ateyya took part in several other initiatives to unite the left, including a 2005 attempt to rally leftist forces under an umbrella organization called the Leftist Union. The initiative ultimately failed due to disagreements among its various factions. In 2005, Ateyya, along with other activists, founded an anti-Mubarak movement similar to the Kefaya movement called the Popular Campaign for Change. This campaign was disbanded in early 2006.

Born in 1951, Ateyya studied at the Engineering Faculty at Cairo University and traveled to the Soviet Union during the mid-seventies to study at Moscow's Petroleum Institute.

Khaled Al-Sayyed
ʿ

Khaled Al-Sayyed is a member of the Renewal Socialist Current, one of the main groups that contributed to the founding of the SPA. He was also a member of the Revolution's Youth Coalition Board before it was dissolved in summer 2012, and an active member of the Justice and Freedom Youth Movement. In the parliamentary elections, Al-Sayyed ran in his hometown district of Helwan.

Wael Gamal

Wael Gamal is the Managing Editor of *Al-Shorouk* daily newspaper in Egypt. Gamal is known for his pro-labor and pro-social welfare views. He has written several articles calling for minimum and maximum wages. After the ouster of Mubarak, activists used these articles to refute the government's political attacks against labor protests.

Abdel Ghaffar Shukr

Abdel Ghaffar Shukr is deputy president of the Arab and African Research Center in Cairo and a former member of the Political Bureau of Al-Tagammu Party. He has written several books on Egyptian politics, including *Political Coalitions in Egypt 1976-1993* and *The Role of Civil Society in Democratic Change*.

Amr Abdel Rahman

Amr Abdel Rahman is one of the founding members of the SPA. Born in 1980, Abdel Rahman is a former political analyst for the European Union Commission in Cairo and currently a researcher at Essex University in the United Kingdom. He often criticizes the commitment of the country's mainstream left to classical Marxism. Additionally, Abdel Rahman was one of the founders of the Democratic Left, a group that emerged in 2007 and modeled itself after Europe's social democratic parties.

AL-WAFD PARTY

Al-Wafd Party is one of Egypt's oldest liberal parties. With deposed president Hosni Mubarak's ruling party officially disbanded, Al-Wafd emerged as an influential player in the political arena, commanding the largest network that any political party possesses in Egypt, covering major cities in twenty-four out of twenty-six Egyptian governorates.

With a distinguished group of top Egyptian businessmen on its membership list, Al-Wafd stands out as one of the few established parties that do not face the same financial constraints that have historically challenged many of the country's political parties. The party also enjoys a very strong presence in the media, thanks to its famous daily newspaper, its Internet portal, and a professional, well-equipped media department. Additionally, Al-Wafd's current leader Al-Sayed Al-Badawi is owner of Al-Hayat, one of Egypt's top five television channels. Such are luxuries that very few Egyptian parties possess.

Al-Wafd Party logo. Image from alwafd.org.

Al-Wafd's history dates back to the beginning of party life under the monarchy, making it the oldest among Egypt's existing political parties. The name of the party is Arabic for "The Delegation," and it references Saad Zaghloul's attempt in 1919 to lead a popular delegation to the post-World War I Paris Peace Conference to demand independence for Egypt against the will of British occupation authorities. Threatened by the immense popular support that Zaghloul was able to garner for his mission, British authorities exiled the Egyptian nationalist leader along with members of the prospective delegation to Malta. This move instigated a mass uprising, which led to the 1919 Revolution.

The uprising forced the British authorities to allow Zaghloul and his companions to return to Egypt and to lead a delegation on behalf of the country at the Paris Conference. In Paris, however, Zaghloul and his partners had little luck moving Egypt's case for independence forward. The failure of the delegation prompted the eruption of popular anger against British rule, and occupation authorities responded by sending Zaghloul back into exile. As was the case the first time they tried to exile Zaghloul, British authorities were forced to backtrack on the decision due to tremendous popular pressure.

After returning from his second exile in 1923, Zaghloul and his companions transformed their Paris delegation into a political party carrying the name Al-Wafd. Shortly thereafter, King Fuad I declared Egypt a constitutional monarchy and issued a new constitution that paved the way for forming Egypt's first elected parliament after British recognition of the country's independence. Under Zaghloul's leadership, Al-Wafd Party contested the 1924 election, winning a majority of the seats in parliament. Zaghloul became Egypt's first prime minister under the new constitution, and Al-Wafd Party effectively became one of the cornerstones of the tripartite arrangement that governed Egypt until the 1952 Revolution, which included the palace, British authority, and Al-Wafd.

Months after the 1952 Revolution, Al-Wafd was disbanded along with all other political parties by orders of Egypt's new military rulers, who dissolved all political parties and organizations upon assuming power, sparing only the Muslim Brotherhood (MB), though not for long. In 1978, when President Anwar Sadat allowed the formation of political parties, Al-Wafd was resurrected under the name of the "New Wafd Party."

The New Wafd, now known simply as Al-Wafd, claims to embrace the same principles of the old party. It describes itself as a centrist party that calls for democracy, freedom of speech, and independence of the judiciary. Wafdist media prides itself on the fact that the party was the first to elect Copts to its high-ranking positions. They also note that the party took the initiative to develop and defend the famous crescent and cross emblem, which came to signify unity between Muslims and Copts—a major concern now in Egypt in light of the increasing visibility of Christian-Muslim tensions. As Al-Wafd's founder, Zaghloul is often credited for crystallizing in the memory of Egypt's political community the famous statement, "religion is for God and the nation is for all," which contemporary defenders of secularism in Egypt still invoke. For many observers, Al-Wafd's history obligates its current leaders to defend secular principles against rising political Islamist trends. Thus, the party has faced internal strife every time its leaders have tried to pragmatically form coalitions with the MB.

Al-Wafd's uneasy relationship with the MB goes back to the 1940s. The palace had decided to support the Brotherhood as a means for counterbalancing Al-Wafd, which had tense relations with the palace throughout the 1930s and 1940s. By the end of the 1940s, competition between the two groups intensified as the MB began challenging Al-Wafd's long-standing dominance inside the political arena.

The 1952 Revolution brought that rivalry to an end—at least temporarily—as Egypt's new military rulers disbanded all political parties, including Al-Wafd. While the Free Officers initially spared the Muslim Brotherhood from that decision and allowed it to operate for a while, Gamal Abdel Nasser eventually banned the MB in 1954 as relations between the two soured.

The MB and Al-Wafd returned to the political scene following President Anwar Sadat's decision to transform Egypt's one-party system into a limited multi-party one. Sadat allowed MB leaders to resume their work in the 1970s, and thus the MB was resurrected after a more-than-two-decades absence. Under Mubarak, the Brotherhood was generally allowed to participate in political life without an official legal status, though the degree to which the Mubarak regime tolerated the group's activism varied over time. It was only after the January 25 Revolution that the Brotherhood was able to establish a licensed political party, namely the Freedom and Justice Party (FJP). After its initial attempt to regroup faced state-imposed hurdles, Al-Wafd was finally able to reestablish itself as an official party through a 1984 court order.

In the lead-up to the 1984 parliamentary elections, the MB and Al-Wafd formed an electoral coalition in an attempt to counterbalance the dominance of the ruling National Democratic Party (NDP). The two groups managed to win fifty-eight seats in the 458-member parliament. Soon after, relations between the Brotherhood and Al-Wafd soured and their cooperation became limited. Wafdists claim that the Brotherhood reneged on its promise to ensure that any Brotherhood members elected through Al-Wafd's list would caucus with the party's bloc in parliament.

During Mubarak's last decade in office, Al-Wafd and other licensed opposition parties were repeatedly accused of striking deals with the Mubarak regime at the expense of the MB. Some contend that the former regime used to rig certain electoral races in favor of Al-Wafd candidates in order to undermine the Brotherhood's standing among opposition forces. Interestingly, Al-Wafd officials have charged that the MB agreed to a "deal" with the Mubarak regime in the 2005 parliamentary elections, contending that the regime allowed the Brotherhood to win eighty-eight seats in order to undermine and threaten liberal opposition groups that disagree with the MB's Islamist agenda.

Relations between the Brotherhood and Al-Wafd saw relative improvement after the election of Al-Sayed Al-Badawi as chair of the latter party in 2010. Cooperation between the two groups became more visible that same year. This was to the dismay of many Wafdists who view their party's cooperation with an Islamist group like the Brotherhood as a violation of the party's secular principles. For example, in 2010 Al-Wafd's official Sameh Makram Ebeid, a member of a prominent Wafdist family, resigned from the party on grounds that Al-Badawi's attempts to enhance cooperation with the MB at the time were undermining Al-Wafd's long-standing secular identity. Ebeid claimed that Al-Badawi tried to appease the Brotherhood by removing from Al-Wafd's publications the "crescent and cross" emblem, widely seen as the symbol of Muslim-Christian unity in Egypt. Al-Wafd's unsuccessful attempt to form an electoral coalition with the MB in the lead-up to the 2011/2012 parliamentary elections revived similar concerns among its members and prompted internal divisions and some defections.

Before the Revolution

Despite its rich history, Al-Wafd Party was not thought of as a major political player before the January 25 Revolution. It frequently adopted stances that supported Mubarak's National Democratic Party (NDP), and is said to have struck deals with the regime in exchange for a few parliamentary seats.

Former Al-Wafd leader Noaman Gomaa was a presidential candidate in the 2005 election, which many viewed as little more than window dressing for an autocratic regime. When a majority of other parties decided to boycott the elections, Gomaa's candidacy came across as selling out. Al-Wafd, the story went, was giving credibility to the elections in exchange for a handful of parliamentary seats.

In the 2005 elections, wherein the MB won eighty-eight parliamentary seats, Al-Wafd only won six. In the presidential election of the same year, Gomaa finished third after Mubarak and Ayman Nour of the then-newly formed Al-Ghad Party. A former Wafdist, Nour had left the party four years earlier due to disagreements with Gomaa. Nour's campaign was widely seen as credible and courageous, whereas observers did not take Gomaa's campaign seriously.

In the 2010 parliamentary elections, Al-Wafd was once again accused of underhanded dealings with the NDP, which ended up dominating the vote through widespread fraud. Most opposition parties, including Al-Wafd, were initially poised to boycott the 2010 elections, but Al-Wafd broke ranks and began fielding candidates. Soon afterward, the MB and others followed suit. Al-Wafd was thus accused of sabotaging the prospective boycott. Many prominent figures were calling on parties to boycott the poll in order to pressure the Mubarak regime into allowing independent candidates who were not handpicked by the NDP a fair chance at getting their names on the ballot in the 2011 presidential election. The party's decision to participate, therefore, angered many young political activists who demonstrated in front of the party's headquarters, causing the party a great deal of embarrassment.

In December 2010, less than two months ahead of the January 25 Revolution, Al-Wafd leader Al-Sayed Al-Badawi decided that the party would withdraw from the parliamentary elections. Al-Wafd had already won two seats in the first round, but Al-Badawi said that his party was going to boycott the run-offs in protest of what he described as electoral fraud. He added that Al-Wafd "wants to stand by the people and not by a deceitful parliament." Many of the party's candidates who qualified for the run-off races disregarded Al-Badawi's directive to boycott the poll and participated anyway.

At the time, Ahmed Ezz, the NDP whip, widely blamed for orchestrating the electoral fraud, denounced the decision. Some say that immense pressure from the party's youth forced Al-Badawi to make this decision.

Al-Badawi was elected leader of Al-Wafd Party earlier in 2010 after Fouad Badrawi, grandson of founder Fouad Serag Al-Din, surprisingly decided not to run for the party's top leadership post.

Earlier in 2006, severe disputes broke out when Al-Wafd leader Gomaa sacked his second-in-command Mounir Fakhry Abdel Nour over the latter's presumed failure to coordinate the party's parliamentary campaign in 2005. When Abdel Nour and his supporters began calling for a "change of leadership," the party's Political Bureau revoked Gomaa's decision to fire Abdel Nour. Al-Wafd Party's Supreme Council subsequently dismissed Gomaa and appointed Mahmoud Abaza as interim leader.

A legal battle ensued, with Gomaa filing a complaint to the prosecutor general against his "illegitimate sacking," saying only the party's General Assembly was entitled to relieve him of his post. To his chagrin, the General Assembly did just that, appointing Mostafa Al-Taweel as interim leader this time.

The strife within the party reached an unexpected climax when Gomaa and his supporters broke into the party's headquarters and opened fire on the rival faction. Nearly twenty-three people were injured in the subsequent battle. Gomaa was arrested in the aftermath of this incident.

After assuming leadership of Al-Wafd, Al-Badawi was able to bring key public figures into the party, including actress Samira Ahmed and poet Ahmed Fouad Negm. Al-Badawi, who made his fortune in the pharmaceutical business, alienated the liberal media when he bought the newspaper *Al-Dostour* and immediately sacked its editor, Ibrahim Eissa, who was one of the most outspoken critics of the Mubarak regime. In the wake of this incident, prominent Wafidist members resigned, including Ahmad Fouad Negm. At the time, critics accused Al-Badawi of doing the "dirty work" of the Mubarak regime.

Similar accusations were leveled against Al-Badawi during the eighteen-day uprising that ultimately resulted in Mubarak's ouster. Al-Badawi's TV station, Al-Hayat, was criticized for siding against the protesters who led the revolution during its early days. Al-Wafd was also criticized for meeting with then-Vice President Omar Suleiman, along with other opposition groups, during the first week of protests in order to negotiate reforms that could mitigate public outrage.

Party Structure

Despite the recurring divisions within its ranks, Al-Wafd prides itself on the strength of its internal structure. The party is run by a supreme council which includes fifty members, all elected by the General Assembly, and is said to be the highest decision making body in the party. The party has branches in twenty-four out of twenty-six Egyptian governorates.

Parliamentary Elections

Al-Wafd was initially slated to contest the parliamentary elections through the Democratic Alliance for Egypt, an electoral coalition formed in mid-June 2011 that includes the MB's Freedom and Justice Party (FJP). In October 2011, Al-Wafd officially withdrew from the alliance, citing disagreements over the selection of candidates.

Prior to Al-Wafd's defection from the Democratic Alliance for Egypt, a spokesman for the latter said that the alliance's aim was "to establish a parliament that is representative of all political forces in society and that would lead to the creation of a national unity government." Critics of the alliance were not convinced. Some pointed out that a merger of the Al-Wafd and the Brotherhood—the two most experienced political groups in the country—was an attempt to dominate the next parliament.

Fielding 570 candidates in the 2011/2012 parliamentary elections, Al-Wafd competed for over eighty percent of the available seats in parliament. Through forty-six lists, the party contested all 332 party list seats available in the 508-member lower house, and presented ninety-six candidates (out of a possible 166) for individual candidacy races in the same chamber. For the 270-member lower house, Al-Wafd presented candidates for 120 (out of a possible 120) party list seats, and contested twenty-two individual candidacy races (out of a possible sixty). Party officials claimed that Copts and women represent 6.5 and ten percent of their candidate rosters, respectively.

The legal framework that governed the 2011/2012 parliamentary elections gave SCAF the right to appoint ten of the 508 members of the lower house, and ninety of the 270 members of the upper house.

Party leader Al-Sayed Al-Badawi disclosed to the media that Al-Wafd's candidate lists are free of ex-NDP members, except for four individuals who were once affiliated with the former ruling party. The disclosure came after many observers had accused Al-Wafd of fielding former ruling party candidates on their electoral lists.

Relationship with Other Political Parties

Many Wafdist figures had publicly criticized their leaders' decision to wage an alliance with the Brotherhood on the grounds that the move made Al-Wafd subservient to a rival organization and compromised the party's long-standing commitment to secular principles, which the Brotherhood opposes. Al-Wafd's officials, however, hold that they left the Democratic Alliance primarily because there was insufficient room in the joint candidate list for the party to field all the candidates it had recruited. It is noteworthy, nonetheless, that Wafdist Wahid Abdel Meguid, the Coordinator of the Democratic Alliance, kept his position in the coalition despite the withdrawal of his party. Abdel Meguid ran in the parliamentary elections on one of the alliance's electoral lists in Cairo.

Stances on Salient Issues

Form of Government

Al-Wafd believes in a parliamentary democracy, in which the power of the parliament exceeds that of the head of state. The party's golden age was all rooted in parliamentary democracy dynamics prior to the revolution of 1952.

Social Justice

Like all parties, Al-Wafd proclaims a commitment to policies that promote social justice, including state-sponsored health care and greater workers' rights.

Economic Policy

Al-Wafd supports a market economy, stable prices, and increased foreign investments. The party opposes monopolistic business practices. Al-Wafd's leader Al-Badawi is famous for being a successful businessman, like many of the party's prominent members.

Religion and State

Since the 1920s, the party has embraced the slogan "religion is for God and the nation is for all." Al-Wafd believes in the separation between religion and state, and has historically advocated for national unity (between Muslims and Copts). Its short-lived alliance with the MB's political party, therefore, seemed perplexing to many observers.

Military Trials

Like most political forces, Al-Wafd Party says it opposes the trial of civilians in military courts. The party, however, boycotted the Tahrir Square demonstration of 9 September 2011, which voiced strong opposition to military trials of civilians.

Strike Law and Labor Movements

Al-Wafd objected to the March 2011 law banning labor strikes and sit-ins. The party, however, did not back this position with a lot of action on the ground, and refrained from joining many activities organized in opposition to this law.

Foreign Relations

In the past, Al-Wafd has been a vocal critic of the Egyptian-Israeli peace treaty. In 2011, its party chair Al-Badawi said that the United States is an obstacle to Arab-Israeli peace due to its bias toward the Israeli side and its blind commitment to protecting Tel Aviv's interests. Al-Badawi has hinted before that annulment of the Camp David Peace Accords is fair game if Israel fails to deliver on its obligations as mandated by the agreement.

Media Image and Controversies

Al-Wafd's alliance with the Muslim Brotherhood—the Democratic Alliance for Egypt that once included over forty parties—was perhaps its most controversial decision since the January 25 Revolution. The FJP's insistence on the implementation of Sharia runs against much of what the liberal Al-Wafd professes to stand for. Ex-parliamentarian Mostafa Al-Guindi and others suspended their membership in Al-Wafd in protest of their party's partnership with the Brotherhood.

Key Figures

Al-Sayed Al-Badawi

Al-Sayed Al-Badawi has served as Al-Wafd Party's leader since 2010. A shrewd businessman who graduated with a pharmacy degree from Alexandria University, Al-Badawi is also the head of Al-Hayat television network and chairman of the board of Sigma, a major pharmaceutical company. His success in securing a TV license from the state prior to the January 25 Revolution raised many questions at the time, as it was believed that the Mubarak regime handed out such licenses only to loyal individuals whom it trusts. Al-Badawi first joined Al-Wafd in 1983 and became secretary general of the party in 2000.

Monir Fakhri Abdel Nour

Mounir Fakhri Abdel Nour is the party's secretary general. He served as minister of tourism in the interim cabinet of Ahmed Shafiq and kept this same post under the government of Essam Sharaf. Abdel Nour is also a successful businessman and former owner of Vitrac, a major food company. He opposed party leader Noaman Gomaa during the acrimonious power struggle of 2006. Abdel Nour was one of the few Wafdist candidates who complied with the party's decision to withdraw from the run-off races during the fraud-ridden parliamentary elections in 2010.

Fouad Badrawi

Fouad Badrawi is the grandson of Fouad Serag El-Din, who brought Al-Wafd back to life in the late 1970s after decades of suspension under the rule of Gamal Abdel Nasser and Anwar Sadat. His unexpected decision not to run for party chair in 2010 paved the way for Al-Badawi to take over that post. He is now one of the party's several high-ranking secretaries.

Mostafa Al-Guindi

Mostafa Al-Guindi is a businessman and former parliamentarian who joined Al-Wafd in 2010. He suspended his membership in Al-Wafd in protest of his party's alliance with the MB, saying that Al-Wafd was wrong to associate itself with a religious-leaning group. He was one of the organizers of the post-revolution visits to Nile Basin countries by an Egyptian popular delegation.

AL-WASAT PARTY

Al-Wasat Party was formed in 1996, well before Egypt's January 25 Revolution. It was denied license four times until it was formally recognized as a legal political party by court order a week after Hosni Mubarak's ouster in February 2011. The Al-Wasat Party has often been portrayed to be a moderate Islamist alternative to the Muslim Brotherhood (MB).

Before the Revolution

Al-Wasat's founders include several MB defectors, most notably Abul Ela Madi, who currently heads the party. Al-Wasat has consistently denied allegations that it was formed as a result of directives from the Brotherhood's Guidance Bureau. Other prominent individuals who have been tied to Al-Wasat over the years include the late Abd Al-Wahab Al-Mesiri, who was once the coordinator of the Kefaya movement, former presidential candidate Mohamed Selim Al-Awa, and former prominent Brotherhood member Essam Sultan.

Al-Wasat Party logo. Image from alwasatparty.com

The party has had a long history of opposing the former regime, particularly its "presidential inheritance" plan to directly pass on the presidency from Mubarak to his son, Gamal Mubarak. Al-Wasat's leaders played a leading role in forming the Kefaya movement and were active members in it. Founded in 2004, Kefaya was the first opposition movement to demand that Mubarak step down as Egypt's president. Al-Wasat's leaders were also active in the National Association for Change reform movement, which was formed in 2010 and called for democratic reforms such as free and fair presidential elections allowing independent candidates to run without being handpicked by the Mubarak regime.

Party Structure

A chair and a thirty-member Supreme Council are responsible for running the party, both elected by a General Assembly. The Political Bureau is responsible for overseeing the implementation of council decisions and may pass decisions if the Supreme Council is unable to convene.

Parliamentary Elections

Al-Wasat Party participated in the parliamentary elections without being part of any formal electoral coalition. Through forty-six lists, the party contested all 332 party list seats available in the 508-member lower house of parliament. Additionally, Al-Wasat fielded seventy (out of a possible 166) candidates for individual candidacy seats in the same chamber. For the 270-member upper house, the party contested twenty-four (out of a possible thirty) party-list races through ninety-six (out of a possible 120) candidates, and ran in twenty (out of a possible sixty) individual candidacy races. The legal framework that governed the 2011/2012 elections gave SCAF the right to appoint ten of the 508 members of the lower house, and ninety of the 270 members of the upper house.

Al-Wasat Party leader Abul Ela Madi announced that the party's candidate roster contains sixty-nine women and two Copts. The party's electoral lists also included five candidates from Al-Nahda Party and eight from Al-Riyada Party, both of which were founded by former members of the MB.

Prominent figures among Al-Wasat's candidates in the 2011/2012 election included party cofounder Essam Sultan who headed the party's list in his hometown of Damietta. Al-Wasat's list in Miniya, headed by party leader Madi, entered an extremely competitive race against the Freedom and Justice list headed by Saad Al-Katatny. Al-Katatny is the Secretary General of the Freedom and Justice Party, founded by the MB, the same group from which Madi defected in the 1990s. Ultimately, Madi lost the race, and Al-Katatny won and became the speaker of the lower house of parliament.

Madi has said Al-Wasat's electoral platform focuses on the underlying political situation and the most pressing economic challenges, particularly unemployment.

Relationship with Other Political Parties

Al-Wasat Party was once a participant in the Democratic Alliance for Egypt but withdrew due to what party leaders described as the MB's domineering role in the alliance. Abul Ela Madi claims that the Socialist Popular Alliance, Al-Adl, and Al-Karama parties turned down Al-Wasat's proposal to form a "third-way" electoral coalition.

Being a splinter group of former Muslim Brotherhood members, Al-Wasat Party has had a tense relationship with the Brotherhood since its creation. Al-Wasat has always presented its long plight to form Al-Wasat Party as a struggle against both Mubarak's regime and the MB. Party leader Madi has been an outspoken critic of the Brotherhood's centralized decision-making style and iron-clad discipline. In a 2000 *Ahram Weekly* interview, Madi further criticized the MB for escalating tensions between Islamists and the state by being too confrontational and insisting on contesting elections. In the same interview, Madi stated that he would support "competent candidates," including some fielded by Mubarak's ruling National Democratic Party.

Over the years, leaders from Al-Wasat and the MB have exchanged attacks through media outlets. In 2010, party leader Essam Sultan accused the Muslim Brotherhood of trying to control the National Association for Change and use the organization to promote its own candidates before the 2010 legislative elections. In 2011, Madi accused the Brotherhood of "swallowing up the Democratic Alliance for Egypt," referring to what he viewed as the group's dominance over the coalition's electoral lists. He also asserted that the Freedom and Justice Party is fully subservient to the Brotherhood, despite the party's attempts to appear independent.

Al-Wasat's leaders have historically had good relations with non-Islamist opposition figures, as evidenced by their prominent role in Kefaya and the National Association for Change, which were once celebrated as rare examples of cooperation between Islamist and secular-leaning activists in Egypt.

Stances on Salient Issues

Social Justice

Al-Wasat's platform states that the absence of social justice in Egypt is not due to a poor distribution of existing wealth, but rather a lack of socioeconomic development in impoverished communities. Accordingly, the state should not combat poverty through wealth redistribution but instead through subsidized public services and local development programs aimed at raising the incomes of underprivileged households. The party advocates for setting a minimum wage that is linked to inflation and enforceable in both public and private sectors.

Economic Policy

The party believes free markets are integral to Egypt's economic well-being, though it supports state intervention in maintaining public infrastructure, promoting social justice, protecting the environment, and protecting against monopolistic practices.

Religion and State

Al-Wasat describes itself as a "civil" party with an "Islamic frame of reference" that nevertheless opposes theocratic rule. The platform describes Islam not only as a religion but also as a civilization and culture. This view is considered to be consistent with a civil democratic state. The party further opposes discrimination based on religion and professes to support religious freedom.

In 2000, party leader Madi founded a nonprofit organization, the Egyptian Association for Dialogue and Culture, aimed at fostering Muslim-Christian dialogue. Madi claims that Al-Wasat has many Coptic members.

Military Trials

Al-Wasat opposes the practice of trying civilian suspects in military courts and party members themselves were victims of military trials in the mid-1990s. The party was an official participant in the 30 September 2011 Tahrir Square demonstration dubbed the "Friday of Reclaiming the Revolution," which included a demand to cease all military trials of civilians. Al-Wasat signed a statement with seventeen other parties and three presidential candidates to oppose the persistence of both military trials and emergency law.

Strike Law and Labor Movements

Al-Wasat professes support for workers' right to strike but does not support "non-peaceful" labor action that result in hindering economic production and business operations. Party leader Madi told *Akhbar Al-Youm*: "There are two types of sit-ins. One is peaceful like the ones that happen on Fridays and thus do not hinder work or hurt production. And these present a healthy phenomenon. As for sit-ins that result in blocking streets and obstructing production, these are harmful and result in negative effects on the economy."

Foreign Relations

The party supports the right of the Palestinian people to an independent state with Jerusalem as its capital, as well as their right of return. It recognizes the right of Palestinians to resist Israeli occupation by any means necessary, including force of arms. Al-Wasat calls for greater parity in Egypt's relations with the United States, arguing that this is the key to a stronger US-Egyptian relationship.

Media Image and Controversies

Despite a long history of cooperation with non-Islamist groups, the Al-Wasat Party faced-off with many such groups after Mubarak's ouster due to disagreements over SCAF-proposed constitutional amendments, which seventy-seven percent of Egyptian voters approved on 19 March 2011. Liberal and leftist activists opposed these amendments on the grounds that they failed to overhaul the "authoritarian constitution" inherited from the Mubarak era, whereas Al-Wasat's leaders, along with other Islamist groups, claimed that approving these amendments was the best way to ensure a swift end to military rule.

Internal differences inside Al-Wasat went public when party activists criticized their leaders' endorsement of Mohamed Selim Al-Awa's bid for the presidency. Dissenting members claim that this decision was made without any deliberation. Alternatively, many party members supported the presidential candidacy of rival Abdel Moneim Abul Futtoh. Al-Wasat later announced that it would try to convince Al-Awa and Abul Futtoh to agree on withdrawing one of their candidacies in order to offer voters a single voice for "moderate Islamism." Eventually, the two candidates ran in the presidential election and Al-Wasat chose to endorse Abul Futtoh.

In 2010, Al-Awa was accused of inciting hatred against Egypt's Coptic community, following televised comments in which he suggested that Coptic churches were stockpiling weapons. Al-Awa denies he ever made such a statement and claims his comments were taken out of context.

Key Figures

Abul Ela Madi

Born in 1958, Abul Ela Madi is Al-Wasat Party's leader and one of its most prominent cofounders. In the 2011/2012 parliamentary elections, Madi ran for a lower house seat in his hometown of Minya, facing off against prominent MB leader Saad Al-Katatni. Before forming Al-Wasat, he was an active member of the Brotherhood, but left the group due to disagreements over forming a political party. Madi was hauled before a military tribunal alongside other party founders for allegedly trying to form a political party as a front for an "illegal organization." He was later acquitted.

Earlier in 1979, while in prison for his political activism at Minya University, Madi joined the Brotherhood. Beforehand, he was a member of the Islamic Group (Al-Gamaa Al-Ismaliyya). Madi won consecutive student union elections at Minya University from 1977 to 1979. From 1987 to 1995, Madi was deputy secretary general of the Engineers' Syndicate. He ran for a parliamentary seat in Helwan in 1995 and obtained a law degree in 2008. Madi is author of a number of works on Islamic thought.

Mohamed Selim Al-Awa

Born in 1944, Mohamed Selim Al-Awa is an Islamic intellectual and judicial expert. He graduated from the Faculty of Law at Alexandria University and obtained a PhD in comparative law from London University. His published works include titles such as *Political Systems in Islam* and *Egypt's Political and Constitutional Crisis*. Al-Awa was Al-Wasat's legal representative in its long battle for an official party license. He ran in the 2012 presidential election, but lost.

Essam Sultan

Essam Sultan is a prominent lawyer and Al-Wasat's deputy leader. Along with Abul Ela Madi, Sultan abandoned the Brotherhood to establish Al-Wasat. He is also a member of the Kefaya movement. Born in 1964, Sultan graduated from Cairo University's faculty of law in 1986.

Meet the NDP Offshoots

The National Democratic Party (NDP) of ousted president Hosni Mubarak was dissolved on 16 April 2011 by the Supreme Administrative Court's order.

Since then, former NDP officials have established what are generally considered as offshoots of the disbanded party. At least six such parties have been formed in the lead-up to the 2011/2012 parliamentary elections.

Freedom Party (Hizb al-Horreya)

The Freedom Party was founded on 17 July 2011 and is led by party chair Mamdouh Hassan and secretary general Moatz Hassan, who are brothers. Their father, Mohammad Mahmoud Ali Hassan, is a construction magnate who used to chair the Housing Committee of the parliament's lower house under Mubarak's rule.

The official Political Parties' Registration Committee initially rejected the Freedom Party's application for a license, but a court order later reversed that decision and granted the party legal status. As of late 2011, the Freedom Party claimed about 15,000 members who are mostly from the Upper Egyptian governorates of Qena and Luxor. The party fielded more than 500 candidates in the elections.

Egyptian Citizen Party (Hizb al-Mowaten al-Masri)

Led by construction magnate Alaa Hasaballah, the Egyptian Citizen Party was founded on 31 July 2011. Among its 15,000 members, the party has several former NDP officials and ministers, including Mohamed Ragab, who briefly served as the NDP's general secretary after the January 25 Revolution. According to Hasaballah, the party fielded more than 450 candidates in the elections.

National Party of Egypt (Hizb Masr Al-Qawmi)

The National Party of Egypt was founded on 17 August 2011 by the late Talaat Al-Sadat, nephew of the late president Anwar Sadat and a former People's Assembly member. Al-Sadat, who passed away on 20 November 2011, served as the NDP's leader for a few days before the party was disbanded on 16 April 2011. The party's 10,000 members include former NDP officials from Menoufia (the birthplace of Al-Sadat's family) and Daqahliyya. Tawfik Okasha, another influential member, is a famous TV show presenter and owner of the private television channel Faraeen (Pharaohs), which was closely tied to the former regime. The National Egypt Party fielded candidates in most of Egypt's Nile-delta governorates.

Modern Egypt Party (Hizb Masr al-Haditha)

The Modern Egypt Party was formed on 3 July 2011. Its founder, Nabil Dibis, is a former member of the defunct NDP and owner of Modern Egypt, a private university. Walid Dibis, Nabil's son, is the owner of the Modern Egypt television channels, which were closely associated with the former regime. The Dibis family used to be a major sponsor of the NDP's weekly newspaper *Al-Watani Al-Youm* (the NDP Today). According to Dibis, the party has more than 15,000 members and fielded candidates in seventeen governorates in the 2011/2012 parliamentary elections.

Union Party (Hizb al-Ittihad)

The Union Party was founded on 18 September 2011. Hossam Badrawi, the party's founder, briefly served as secretary-general of the NDP in the last days of Mubarak's rule. Badrawi was perceived by some as a reformist, despite his close ties to Gamal Mubarak. He left the NDP just one day before Mubarak resigned on 11 February 2011. The party claims 15,000 members and fielded 500 candidates in the parliamentary elections.

Beginning Party (Hizb al-Bedaya)

The Beginning Party was founded on 3 August 2011, and many of its 6,000 members are former affiliates of the dismantled NDP. Mahmoud Hossameddin Galal, the party's founder, is a prominent businessman. The Beginning Party's founding members are said to include Egyptians living abroad. Many individuals challenged the party's initial bid for a license on grounds that its founding members include NDP leaders.

Conservatives Party (Hizb al-Mohafizin)

The Conservatives Party's founder, Akmal Qortam, ran as an NDP candidate in the Cairo district of Maadi in the 2010 parliamentary elections, which were marred with widespread fraud and violence. Qortam is owner of Sahara, a major oil exploration company. During the lead-up to the 2011/2012 legislative elections, Qortam had announced that the party would contest sixty percent of the seats in parliament.

Egypt Development Party (Hizb Masr al-Tanmiya)

Egypt Development Party founder Youmna al-Hamaki served as a member of the parliament's lower house. Al-Hamaki was a member of the NDP's Policies Committee. She is a professor of economics at Cairo University.

Egypt Revival Party (Hizb Masr al-Nahda)

The former NDP's prominent businessman Hossam Badrawi, who founded the Ittihad party, is the main backer of the Egypt Revival Party. The Egypt Revival Party mainly draws its membership from young former NDP members.

Egypt Renaissance Party (Hizb Nahdet Masr)

The Egypt Renaissance Party was founded by Ahmed Abul-Nazar, a prominent businessman. Abul-Nazar was an NDP candidate in the 2010 parliamentary elections in the Alexandria district of Al-Raml. Most of the party's members are former NDP officials from Alexandria.

2 | Coalitions

Democratic Alliance for Egypt

Coalition Members: Freedom and Justice Party, Al-Karama Party, Ghad Al-Thawra Party, Labor Party, Al-Islah wal-Nahda Party, Al-Hadara Party, Al-Islah Party, Al-Geel Party, Misr Al-Arabi Al-Ishtiraki Party, Al-Ahrar Party, Al-Horiyya wal-Tanmiya Party.

In early June 2011, a group of twenty-eight Egyptian political parties joined forces to form the Democratic Alliance for Egypt for the purpose of coordinating their electoral strategies for Egypt's first legislative elections following the ouster of former president Hosni Mubarak. The alliance's founding statement, dated 14 June 2011, stated that alliance members would seek to mobilize political forces that are committed to the principles of democracy and a civil state, and to secure a representative parliament that would lead to a government of national unity.

The Democratic Alliance was the first electoral coalition to emerge in post-Mubarak Egypt. Since every party was invited to join the alliance, it remained unclear for a while which parties or groupings it would compete against in the elections. Other coalitions later sprang up, clarifying the contours of the electoral map.

After experiencing multiple defections and entries, as of late October 2011, the alliance comprises eleven parties, most notably the Freedom and Justice Party (FJP), the political party of the Muslim Brotherhood (MB), which dominated the alliance's electoral lists. Ghad Al-Thawra and Al-Karama parties remained the only significant partners to the FJP in the Democratic Alliance. The coalition at its high point included over forty parties. The Democratic Alliance for Egypt was generally seen as the Brotherhood's alliance. The alliance did not run under the MB's controversial slogan "Islam is the Solution," but rather "We bear good for all of Egypt."

The alliance presented candidates for almost all the available seats in the People's Assembly, the parliament's 508-member lower house. Eleven parties were scheduled to contest the parliamentary elections through the alliance's joint candidate lists. The FJP topped over sixty percent of the alliance's forty-six electoral lists, and contested over seventy percent of individual candidacy seats. The FJP fielded over 500 candidates for the two parliamentary chambers, and Al-Karama Party nominated sixteen candidates, including three for individual candidacy seats, while Ghad Al-Thawra nominated fifteen candidates. In total, 678 parliamentary seats were up for grab in the election (498 in the lower house and 180 in the upper house). The legal framework that governed the 2011/2012 parliamentary elections gave SCAF the right to appoint ten of the 508 members of the lower house, and ninety of the 270 members of the upper house.

The alliance once included long-standing opposition parties, such as the century-old liberal Al-Wafd Party, the socialist Al-Tagammu, and the Nasserist Party. It also comprised parties that were either formed or legalized after Mubarak's downfall, like the nationalist Al-Karama Party, the Islamist Al-Wasat Party, the Egypt Freedom Party, and the Salafist Al-Nour Party. Most of these parties left the coalition.

Initially, alliance members coalesced around the concern that ex-regime figures and associates could easily secure parliamentary representation at their expense, absent electoral coordination among opposition groups. The alliance, however, faced internal splits soon after.

The combination of a strong Islamist trend in the coalition alongside a liberal one challenged the ideological and political coherence of the grouping. Less than a month following the formation of the alliance, defections began mounting. The Democratic Front Party withdrew on grounds that a partnership with Islamist groups is inconsistent with the party's liberal principles. The Front, however, did not explain why it joined an alliance that clashed with its principles in the first place.

The leftist Al-Tagammu announced it would exit the coalition in the wake of a controversy, in which activists affiliated with Islamist members of the alliance instigated strife at the demonstrations held on 29 July 2011 under the banner "The Friday of Unity and Popular Will." The Friday demonstrations were initially aimed at emphasizing national unity and, among other things, the need to cease military trials of civilians. Al-Tagammu alleged that Islamist activists failed to adhere to the demonstrations' formal demands—which were agreed to in advance—and instead decided to promote divisive slogans calling for the establishment of an "Islamic state" and the implementation of Sharia law. The Islamist organizations responsible for propagating these slogans on 29 July denied having agreed to any set of collective demands prior to the demonstration.

Ideological and political rifts once again challenged the cohesion of the alliance when some Wafdist leaders announced they would leave the group, citing among other things, reservations about Al-Wafd's alliance with the MB. Many Wafdist figures had publicly criticized their leaders' decision to form an alliance with the Brotherhood on grounds that the move made Al-Wafd subservient to a rival organization and compromised the party's long-standing commitment to secular principles, which the Brotherhood opposes. The defectors, Alaa Abdel Monem, Mostafa Al-Guindi, and Mona Makram Ebeid joined the Egyptian Bloc, a rival electoral coalition founded by secular-leaning parties.

Al-Wafd ultimately withdrew from the alliance in October 2011, citing disagreements with the FJP over the relative positions of their respective candidates on the alliance's joint lists. While some observers attribute this split to the incompatibility of Al-Wafd's secular sensibilities and the Muslim Brotherhood's Islamist agenda, Al-Wafd's officials hold that they left the Democratic Alliance primarily because there was insufficient room on the joint electoral lists for the party to field all the candidates it had recruited.

While the Islamist/secular divide has undermined unity inside the Democratic

Alliance, non-Islamist parties, like the liberal Ghad Al-Thawra and the nationalist Al-Karama, have remained in the coalition alongside the FJP, and contested the elections through the Democratic Alliance.

Political differences also loomed large in stirring division inside the alliance. For instance, Al-Adl (Justice) Party withdrew from the coalition at an early stage on the grounds that it did not wish to cooperate with traditional opposition groups that were loyal to the previous regime and that benefited from its largesse. The alliance encompassed several parties that were pejoratively dubbed "paper parties" during the Mubarak era, in reference to the insignificance of their role.

The Egypt Freedom Party, a liberal party led by Amr Hamzawy, announced it would leave the alliance because its participants did not seem serious about developing consensus among its member organizations on the principles that would guide constitution-drafting efforts. The Egypt Freedom Party later co-founded the "Egyptian Bloc," which it left before ultimately choosing to field candidates through the Revolution Continues Alliance.

Internal differences persisted in the alliance and it was later on the side of the Islamists that disagreements started to simmer. The Salafist Al-Nour Party left the Democratic Alliance in September, citing its marginalization in the coalition's decision-making vis-à-vis liberal parties. Observers believe, however, that Al-Nour left the alliance once it became clear that its candidates would not top the coalition's joint electoral lists.

This particular withdrawal had a major impact on the alliance. In the week that followed, two other Salafist parties, Al-Asala and Al-Fadila, withdrew, followed later by the Building and Development Party, the party established by the Islamic Group (Al-Gamaa Al-Islamiyya).

The Nasserist Party followed suit days later over disagreements with the FJP, objecting to its dominant position in the alliance's lists.

A political rift between the Salafists and the Muslim Brotherhood became evident after Al-Nour Party formed the Islamist Bloc, an electoral coalition that included two other Islamist parties, Al-Asala and Building and Development. The Islamist Bloc (also known as the Alliance for Egypt) competed with the Democratic Alliance for the votes of pro-Islamist constituents. The Brotherhood and the Salafist Al-Nour Party, moreover, signed a document that committed both sides to clean and fair competition in their electoral face-off, though it is unclear why other parties were not included in the agreement.

Caught between the new Islamist parties and the secular blocs, the FJP tried to recruit prominent independent candidates from outside the MB to run on its lists. For example, party leaders have reportedly asked Hassan Nafaa to run on one of their electoral lists in Cairo. Nafaa is a prominent political scientist, public figure, and former coordinator of Mohamed ElBaradei's National Association for Change. FJP initially assured him that he would not have to officially join the party in order to run on its electoral lists. According to Nafaa, however, after accepting the FJP's offer, the party reneged on its promise and asked that he fill out a membership application in order to process the paperwork for his candidacy. Nafaa took the matter to the press, implicitly accusing the MB of opportunism.

Egyptian Bloc

Coalition Members: Free Egyptians Party, the Egyptian Social Democratic Party, Al-Tagammu Party.

The Egyptian Bloc consisted of the Free Egyptians Party, the Egyptian Social Democratic Party, and Al-Tagammu Party. The bloc was often portrayed as a "secular-leaning" alliance that sought to counterbalance the influence of the Muslim Brotherhood in the 2011/2012 elections, specifically the Brotherhood-led Democratic Alliance's electoral coalition. Members of the bloc announced in early November 2011 that their partnership is not simply a short-term electoral coalition, but encompasses a long-term political alliance aimed at turning Egypt into a civil democratic state.

The Egyptian Bloc fielded 412 candidates for the parliamentary lower house elections. The bloc contested all 332 party list seats available in the 508-member lower house, in addition to fielding eighty (out of a possible 166) candidates for individual candidacy races. The legal framework that governed the 2011/2012 parliamentary elections gave the Supreme Council of the Armed Forces the right to appoint ten of the 508 members of the lower house. Half of the bloc's candidates were affiliated with the Free Egyptians Party, forty percent from the Egyptian Social Democratic Party, and ten percent from Al-Tagammu Party.

The Egyptian Bloc at some point included twenty-one political groups. However, following successive defections during the lead up to election, only three parties remained in the bloc by the eve of elections. Defectors include the Egypt Freedom Party, the Socialist Popular Alliance Party (SPA), the Egyptian Socialist Party, the Democratic Front Party, the Tahrir Sufi Party, and others. These parties withdrew from the bloc reportedly due to inter-party conflicts over seat shares and the relative positions of various candidates in the coalition's electoral lists. Disagreements were also associated with allegations that some parties were trying to field ex-members of the former ruling National Democratic Party (NDP) on the bloc's lists to the dismay of member groups that opposed any participation by ex-regime elements in the elections.

The SPA withdrew under these circumstances. The Egyptian Bloc's High Commission for Electoral Coordination denied the allegations, insisting that no former NDP members made their way onto the lists. A Free Egyptian Party official once conceded, however, that the Egyptian Bloc's list included eight former NDP members, but insisted that none of them were engaged in corrupt practices. Amr Hamzawy's Egypt Freedom Party withdrew shortly after, accusing the bloc of a "lack of transparency" in the candidate selection process. The SPA and the Egypt Freedom Party later formed the Revolution Continues Alliance together with the Revolution's Youth Coalition, the Egyptian Current Party, and others. Meanwhile, both the Democratic Front Party and the Tahrir Sufi Party decided to contest the elections alone away from any alliances.

The Egyptian Bloc was aimed at bringing together political forces committed to a civil democratic state based on the separation between religion and politics.

While the Egyptian Bloc was formed to counterbalance the threat posed by the well-organized Islamist camp, Egyptian Social Democratic Party leader Mohamed Abul-Ghar insisted otherwise. He asserted that the bloc was not created to oppose any particular political force, stressing that Islamists were welcome to join the coalition if they shared the specific values espoused by the bloc. However, the fact that the alliance brought together a group of secular leaning parties with opposing economic agendas, such as the socialist Al-Tagammu Party and the pro-business Free Egyptians Party, strongly reinforced this perception.

The press conference launching the Egyptian Bloc's electoral campaign featured strong attacks against the Muslim Brotherhood, Egypt's largest Islamist group and one of the Bloc's major rivals in the parliamentary races. Al-Tagammu Party's Rifaat Al-Said accused the Brotherhood of trying to "hijack Egypt and Egyptians" and said that the group is driven by its goal to dominate politics even if it comes at the expense of national interests. Al-Said is known as a long-standing and vehement critic of Islamist groups.

Under the slogan "together, we will achieve what is ours," the bloc's campaign underscored goals of building a civil democratic state, and promoting economic prosperity through a liberal economy guided by a commitment to social justice. For many observers, however, it is unclear how this unlikely partnership between the Free Egyptians Party, known for its pro-business orientations, and the socialist Al-Tagammu, could possibly yield a meaningful joint vision for the future of Egypt's economy. Since its inception, Al-Tagammu has sought to fight economic liberalization, as well as many aspects of the economic vision that the Free Egyptians espouses.

Islamist Bloc (Alliance for Egypt)

Coalition Members: Al-Nour Party, Al-Asala Party, Building and Development Party.

The Islamist Bloc was an electoral coalition formed by three Islamist political parties with the aim to integrate their efforts in the 2011/2012 parliamentary elections. The Islamist Bloc was comprised of the Salafist Al-Nour and Al-Asala Parties, as well as the Building and Development Party, which was founded by the Islamic Group (Al-Gamaa Al-Islamiyya).

Some observers have dubbed this coalition the Islamist Alliance. The three parties comprising the alliance announced on 3 November 2011 that they would compete in the parliamentary elections under the name of the Alliance for Egypt.

The three parties of the Islamist Bloc were once members of the Democratic Alliance for Egypt, an electoral coalition led by the Freedom and Justice Party of the Muslim Brotherhood. Like many other groups that were once part of the Democratic Alliance, these parties defected in protest of their paltry shares on the Democratic Alliance's joint candidate lists for the parliamentary elections.

A number of other Islamist parties, including Al-Wasat, Labor, Al-Fadila, and

Al-Tawheed Al-Arabi, considered joining the Islamist Bloc after withdrawing from the Democratic Alliance, but ultimately decided against it.

"They did not join us because negotiations with them started too late. There was not enough time to work things out," Nader Bakkar, a member of Al-Nour's Supreme Committee and a party spokesperson, told *Jadaliyya/Ahram Online*. The Labor Party later rejoined the Democratic Alliance.

During the lead-up to the elections, the Islamist Bloc announced it would field 693 candidates in the parliamentary polls, signaling it would contest all 678 seats that were up for grabs (498 in the lower house and 180 in the upper house). On its part, Al-Nour contributed 610 candidates to the coalition's electoral rosters, which included 477 candidates for the parliament's lower house and 133 candidates for the upper house. Al-Asala and Building and Development competed for only forty and forty-five seats, respectively, leaving more than eighty-five percent of the joint candidate roster to Al-Nour. Earlier in the election season, Al-Nour Party's spokesperson once refused to specify the proportion of seats contested by each of the three parties of the coalition on grounds that Al-Nour did not want to belittle the role of its two coalition partners. The legal framework that governed the 2011/2012 parliamentary elections gave SCAF the right to appoint ten of the 508 members of the lower house, and ninety of the 270 members of the upper house.

While the Islamist Bloc's electoral lists included women, they did not include Copts. Al-Nour once stated that it would consider fielding Coptic candidates, as long as those candidates represent the party's platform.

Al-Nour Party is the largest and the first Salafist political party to be registered in Egypt. It is linked to Al-Daawa Movement (or Al-Daawa Al-Salafiyya), a Salafist group based in Alexandria. Al-Nour's co-founders include renowned Salafist cleric Yasser Borhami, whose stature enhanced the party's fame and weight among the Islamists. It was widely reported that Borhami discouraged Al-Daawa Movement's supporters from participating in the 25 January demonstrations, which ultimately escalated into the mass uprising that toppled Hosni Mubarak.

Due to the party's strong roots in Alexandria, it was said that Al-Nour would compete for a considerable number of the parliamentary seats available in that region. Al-Asala Party previously said that it would cede all seats in the governorate of Alexandria to Al-Nour's candidates, whereas Al-Asala's own candidates, including its leader Adel Afifi, would contest electoral races in the Cairo area. Backed by famous Salafist preachers, such as Mohamed Hassan and Mohamed Hussein Yacoub, Al-Asala is another Salafist party that came to light after the January 25 Revolution. It has attracted support from Salafists in the Cairo area.

The Building and Development Party, which fielded candidates on behalf of the Islamist Bloc in Upper Egypt, was formed four months after Mubarak's ouster. It is known as the political arm of the Islamic Group (Al-Gamaa Al-Islamiyya). The group was committed to overthrowing the Egyptian government until its imprisoned leaders renounced violence in 2003. The official Political Parties' Registration Committee had initially refused to license the Building and Development on grounds that it advances a religious program in violation of Egyptian law. The party appealed the decision in court, arguing that it seeks to implement Islamic law in accordance with Article 2 of the constitution, which states that Sharia is the main source of legislation. The court ruled in favor of the Building and Development Party, thereby granting it a license to operate.

In late October 2011, the Islamist Bloc announced plans to wage its electoral campaign under the slogan, "Together, we will build Egypt: A modern identity and state built with Egyptian hands and minds." Al-Nour had pledged to refrain from using religious slogans, or from campaigning inside mosques, in the lead-up to the parliamentary polls, although one party official was once quoted as telling supporters that voting for Al-Nour candidates represented a form of almsgiving that would someday be rewarded in heaven. During the 2011 Eid holiday, moreover, Al-Nour activists competed with those of the MB's Freedom and Justice Party over control of public prayer venues and spaces, as both parties sought to keep their names in the spotlight in religious forums convened during the Muslim holiday.

Al-Nour spokesperson Bakkar said that Al-Nour's campaign motto and its emphasis on "identity" reflect the raison d'être of the Islamist Bloc's parliamentary bid, namely "the application of Sharia [Islamic Law] in a gradual way that suits the nature of society." Bakkar's statement implicitly refers to a common belief among many Islamist activists that Egypt's journey to the complete application of Sharia should be slow and gradual so as not to alienate people. The term "modern state," Bakkar added, signified neither a secular state based on conventional Western understandings nor a fundamentalist religious state, but rather a modern state that relies on science in pursuing progress and prosperity.

The Islamist Bloc's parties' position on women's rights has attracted much attention since its inception. While Al-Nour's platform states that men and women are equal with respect to human dignity, it underscores "the importance of maintaining differences in their human and social roles." At a press conference announcing the Building and Development Party's formation, an Al-Gamaa Al-Islamiyya spokesperson told reporters: "Islam guarantees women their appropriate and sufficient rights. [Former first lady] Suzanne Mubarak gave women [in Egypt] more than their lawful rights and that is not acceptable."

The Islamist Bloc's announcement that it would field sixty female candidates in the elections became the source of considerable controversy, since many Salafists do not believe that women should vote, let alone run for office. In response, Al-Nour leader at the time Emad Abd Al-Ghafour stressed that the party was committed to the principle that men and women should not mingle, and that the decision to field female candidates had been a necessary measure aimed at winning as many seats as possible, given that the law stipulates a set quota for female candidates on party lists. Al-Ghafour went on to note, however, that female candidates would remain at the tail end of the list and would therefore have very little chance of securing representation.

Al-Nour Party, the largest group in the Islamist Bloc, tried to repair its image vis-à-vis women's rights by convening a convention for its female activists. The party's detractors, however, cynically mocked this initiative, pointing out that none of the speakers at the event were women, but rather a handful of old men lecturing female attendees about the nature and scope of their political rights.

Al-Nour was also criticized for refusing to include photos of its female candidates alongside those of its male nominees in its electoral flyers, simply inserting the image of a flower above the names of women running on the party's lists.

During the lead-up to the vote, spokesperson Bakkar said that the Islamist Bloc would rely on an international marketing company to design its campaign ads, stressing that none of the candidates affiliated with the coalition would spend more than the legally mandated campaign-spending cap of 500,000 EGP.

Facing competition in Upper Egyptian governorates from affiliates of Mubarak's now-defunct National Democratic Party (NDP) and its offshoots, particularly those hailing from powerful and well-connected Upper Egyptian families, Al-Nour had unveiled plans to launch voter awareness campaigns and mount legal challenges against those candidates once tied to the former regime.

Prior to the vote, the Muslim Brotherhood and Al-Nour had signed a joint document committing both sides to "clean and fair competition" in their electoral faceoff, though it is unclear why other parties were not included in the agreement. Nevertheless, the two Islamist coalitions competed fiercely over votes cast by Islamist constituents who previously had little choice but to vote for the MB.

REVOLUTION CONTINUES ALLIANCE

Coalition Members: The Socialist Popular Alliance Party, the Egyptian Socialist Party, the Egyptian Current Party, the Egypt Freedom Party, Equality and Development Party, the Revolution's Youth Coalition, the Egyptian Alliance Party.

The Revolution Continues (RCA) was an electoral coalition that competed in the 2011/2012 legislative elections, and that, according to its members, comprised an ideologically diverse set of actors, namely liberal, Islamists and socialists, including the youth of the Muslim Brotherhood who defected from the group and helped form the Egyptian Current Party. According to Socialist Popular Alliance Party (SPA) member Abdel Ghaffar Shukr, the RCA stood for freedom, social equality, and human rights. It consisted of the SPA, the Egyptian Socialist Party, the Egyptian Current Party, the Freedom Egypt Party, Equality and Development Party, the Revolution's Youth Coalition (RYC), and the Egyptian Alliance Party.

Through 280 candidates (out of a possible 332), the RCA contested thirty-four (out of a possible forty-six) party list races for the 508-member lower house of parliament. Additionally, twenty-six (out of a possible 166) candidates contested individual candidacy seats. The legal framework that governed the 2011/2012 parliamentary elections gave the Supreme Council of the Armed Forces the right to appoint ten of the 508 members of the lower house.

According to Egyptian Current Party leader and former MB member, Islam Lotfy, 100 of these candidates were below the age of forty. The majority of candidates that the alliance fielded belonged to the SPA, according to RCA member Khaled Abdel Hamid. Some thirty-two were affiliates of the Egyptian Current Party. The

Egypt Freedom Party had announced in late October 2011 plans to field only twenty-two candidates, including party founder Amr Hamzawy who contested and won an individual candidacy seat in Cairo. Two of the coalition's electoral lists featured women in their top spots, namely Karima Al-Hefnawy of the Egyptian Socialist Party and actress Taysir Fahmy of the Equality and Development Party.

Some of the RCA's affiliates who ran for individual-candidacy races were identified on the ballots as "independent" candidates even though they were politically sponsored by the coalition.

Due to much confusion and disagreement, the RCA was formed shortly before the candidate registration deadline. Many of the parties constituting the RCA were initially members of the Egyptian Bloc, a secular leaning alliance that once included the SPA, the Egypt Freedom Party, and the Egyptian Socialist Party. These parties withdrew from the bloc, reportedly due to inter-party conflicts over seat shares and the relative positions of various candidates in the coalition's electoral lists. Disagreements were also associated with allegations that some parties were trying to field ex-members of the former ruling National Democratic Party (NDP) on the bloc's lists to the dismay of member groups that opposed any participation by ex-regime elements in the elections.

Many of the parties that withdrew from the Egyptian Bloc quickly formed the new Revolution Continues Alliance carrying a more socially-oriented agenda. The RYC and the Egyptian Current Party almost withdrew from the RCA one week before the candidate registration deadline, objecting that the SPA was dominating the top positions of all lists at the expense of the youth groups. The problem was quickly renegotiated to allow more youth members to head party lists.

Titled "Security, Freedom, and Social Justice," the RCA's platform, announced in early November 2011, focused on re-establishing law and order, promoting social justice, and closing the income gap between the rich and the poor. According to the platform, members of the alliance, if elected, would work immediately on re-establishing security and cleansing state institutions of corruption — particularly the police, judiciary, state media, and public universities. They would also work on passing a national budget providing for unemployment benefits and increasing state spending on healthcare, education, and public housing. The RCA platform commits its members to providing decent housing conditions to residents of slums, and to establishing a just minimum wage and a maximum wage that does not exceed fifteen times the minimum. The platform called for canceling all debts of small-scale farmers and greater protections for the rights of tenant farmers vis-à-vis landowners.

3 | Figures and Actors

Mohamed Abul-Ghar

Mohamed Abul-Ghar is the head of the Egyptian Social Democratic Party, which he co-founded with other activists and public figures after the January 25 Revolution.

In 1962, Abul-Ghar graduated from the Faculty of Medicine at Cairo University and obtained his PhD in 1969, specializing in obstetrics and gynecology. Besides his teaching post at Cairo University, Abul-Ghar pursued an active career in scientific research. He established Egypt's first specialized medical center for assisted fertility in 1986.

Though interested in politics since youth, Abul-Ghar became actively involved in politics during the Mubarak era. In 2004, Abul-Ghar and other university professors founded the 9 March Movement for the Independence of Universities. This group seeks to defend academic freedoms and to protect universities from the intervention of state security agencies, as well as academic corruption and discrimination.

Unwittingly, the group became part of a more general pro-democracy movement, staging its first demonstration months after Kefaya (Enough) protest movement staged theirs against the perpetuation of the Mubarak regime. Nevertheless, the 9 March Movement's dissent has and continues to specifically target conditions and regime practices inside universities.

Before the Revolution

Abul-Ghar was directly involved in anti-regime opposition before the January 25 Revolution. He was a coordinator and spokesperson for the National Association for Change (NAC), which put him on the front lines of political opposition before the revolution erupted in January 2011.

Led by presidential hopeful Mohamed ElBaradei, the NAC was formed in early 2010 as a loose coalition of various political actors who pushed for substantive democratic reforms that would allow viable candidates outside the ruling party, like ElBaradei, a fair shot at contesting in a presidential election. The group was seen at the time as an attempt by opposition forces to resist apparent efforts by the former regime to groom Mubarak's influential son, Gamal Mubarak, as his father's presidential successor.

Prior to the beginning of mass protests in January 2011, Abul-Ghar's anti-regime tone was harsh, strongly attacking the state after church bombings killed tens of people in Alexandria on New Year's Eve.

That January, he joined a group of ex-members of parliament, public figures, and youth representatives to form a "parallel parliament," shadowing the work of Egypt's actual parliament, which came to power in 2010 through elections that most observers declared fraudulent. This alternative parliament was formed to independently review bills and recommend legislation in parallel to the official one.

The Revolution and Beyond

Mohamed Abul-Ghar participated in the 25 January protests and the eighteen-day uprising, which ended with the toppling of former president Hosni Mubarak. On the first day of protests, Abul-Ghar warned the regime of the tremendous amount of anger that would be unleashed if the government failed to respond with serious reforms, including the dissolution of the parliament and measures to control soaring prices.

After Mubarak's demise, Abul-Ghar helped form the Egyptian Social Democratic Party and became its interim leader. Modeled after European social democratic parties, the party champions social justice and democratic change.

Abul-Ghar continues to be active in the 9 March Movement, supporting student protests, pushing for the removal of deans affiliated with the ex-Mubarak regime, and rejecting continued intervention by government security agencies in university affairs. Abul-Ghar did not run for parliament in the 2011/2012 elections.

Al-Sayed Al-Badawi

Al-Sayed Al-Badawi Shehata (known as Al-Sayed Al-Badawi) is the current leader of Al-Wafd Party. A business tycoon, Al-Badawi has been on Al-Wafd's Higher Committee since 1989. He was Al-Wafd's secretary general before being elected to the party's leadership in 2010.

Graduating from the University of Alexandria's faculty of pharmacy in 1973, Al-Badawi entered the pharmaceuticals industry, where he was able to make a substantial fortune. He founded and is the current chairman and CEO of Sigma Pharmaceutical Industries. In this capacity, Al-Badawi has invested heavily in the Egyptian media. He owns Al-Hayat satellite TV channel, and in 2010 he bought the dissident opposition daily newspaper *Al-Dostour*. Al-Badawi later sold his shares in *Al-Dostour* to his partner, Reda Edward.

Before the Revolution

Al-Badawi's role in the media sector before the start of the January 25 Revolution shaped his image as a public figure.

Considerable controversy over press freedoms arose when Al-Badawi and fellow

Wafdist Reda Edward bought the daily *Al-Dostour* and fired its prominent editor-in-chief Ibrahim Eissa, along with *Al-Dostour*'s editorial team, ahead of the 2010 parliamentary elections. In the wake of this incident, prominent Wafidist members resigned, including poet Ahmad Fouad Negm. At the time, critics accused Al-Badawi of doing the "dirty work" of the Mubarak regime.

Eissa's sharp criticism of the Mubarak regime, and particularly of the potential dynastic succession of Mubarak's son, Gamal, led many to believe that Al-Badawi's takeover of *Al-Dostour* and his nearly instant dismissal of Eissa was part of a deal with the regime. It was widely suggested that in such a deal, Al-Wafd party would win a relatively substantial number of seats in the 2010 elections, thus replacing the Muslim Brotherhood as the main opposition party in the lower house. In return, Al-Badawi would be obliged to use his vast fortune to rid the regime of the "nuisance" represented by Ibrahim Eissa's daily newspaper.

Al-Badawi's announcement at the time that Al-Wafd would secure at least twenty seats in parliament helped confirm that widespread belief. Al-Badawi sold his share in *Al-Dostour* on the same day that Eissa was fired, presumably trying to distance himself from mounting controversy.

However, when the ruling National Democratic Party (NDP) swept the first round of 2010 parliamentary polls, Al-Wafd chose to boycott the runoff elections. Al-Wafd claimed foul play after only two of members won seats in the first round. Many of the party's candidates who qualified for the run-off races disregarded Al-Badawi's directive to boycott the poll and participated anyway.

Al-Badawi's ownership of Al-Hayat satellite TV channel is another source of controversy surrounding Al-Wafd's leader. His success in securing a TV license from the state prior to the January 25 Revolution raised many questions at the time, as it was believed that the Mubarak regime handed out such licenses only to loyal individuals whom it trusts. Before the revolution, the TV channel was believed to be pro-regime. Mahmoud Mosallam, the channel's manager, was purported to enjoy a close relationship with Mubarak's youngest son and once likely heir.

Al-Badawi was elected leader of the Al-Wafd party in 2010, running against former party leader Mahmoud Abaza. His leadership of the party brought an end to a fierce leadership battle between Abaza and his predecessor, Noaman Gomaa, who was Al-Wafd's presidential nominee in 2005.

Although Al-Badawi was critical of the Mubarak regime and a prominent figure in the opposition, he also stated that "no one can deny the legitimacy" of Mubarak's rule a few months before the January 25 Revolution erupted.

The Revolution and Beyond

During the eighteen-day uprising that ousted Mubarak on 11 February 2011, Al-Badawi did not participate in the Tahrir Square sit-in. His TV channel, Al-Hayat, was initially hostile to the anti-Mubarak uprising.

Al-Badawi claims that he approved Al-Wafd youth's participation in the "March of Millions" and other protests during the week that preceded Mubarak's overthrow. Yet, the Revolution's Youth Coalition (RYC), an alliance of some of the Mubarak era's most eminent opposition groups, has openly questioned Al-Wafd's conspicuous absence in the first weeks of the revolution.

The RYC's criticism came after Al-Badawi denounced the 8 July 2011 sit-in, in which dozens of groups took part. Al-Badawi claimed that the sit-in participants had played no role in the January 25 Revolution.

He switched his focus to the parliamentary elections, strongly criticizing electoral laws issued by the ruling Supreme Council of the Armed Forces (SCAF). Al-Badawi warned that these laws could permit the former ruling party, dissolved by court ruling, to resurface on the country's political stage. Interestingly, Al-Badawi later disclosed to the media that Al-Wafd's candidate lists would include four individuals who were once affiliated with the former ruling party. The disclosure came after many observers had accused Al-Wafd of fielding former ruling party candidates on their electoral lists.

Al-Badawi's political experience derives from his career with Al-Wafd Party. He became party secretary in Al-Gharbeya governorate in 1983. In 1989, he was promoted to the supreme council, making him the youngest member in the party's top leadership. Al-Badawi became the party's secretary-general in 2000 and chairman in 2010.

Al-Badawi has stated that Al-Wafd Party's decision to withdraw from the run-off elections in 2010 prompted the Muslim Brotherhood to do the same, and thus drilled the first nail in the Mubarak regime's coffin.

Hossam Badrawi

Hossam Badrawi is a former member of the defunct National Democratic Party (NDP) and served as the former ruling party's secretary-general during President Hosni Mubarak's last days in office. He is also founder of the Union Party, widely seen as one of several NDP offshoots that emerged following the dissolution of the party in April 2011.

Badrawi was born in Cairo in 1953 to a well-established family traditionally affiliated with Egypt's liberal Al-Wafd Party. He graduated from Cairo University's Faculty of Medicine in 1974. In 1983, he earned his PhD in gynecology from Wayne State University in the United States. He currently owns the well-known Nile Badrawi Hospital in Cairo's Maadi neighborhood.

Badrawi entered Egyptian political life in the second half of the 1990s. He joined then-president Hosni Mubarak's ruling National Democratic Party (NDP) in 2000, alongside presidential scion Gamal Mubarak; business tycoon Ahmed Ezz (later NDP secretary for organizational affairs); Mahmoud Mohieddin (later investment minister); Youssef Boutros-Ghali (later finance minister); and Rachid Mohamed Rachid (later trade and industry minister).

In 2000, the NDP fielded Badrawi in elections for the lower house of Egypt's parliament, the People's Assembly, for Cairo's downtown Qasr El-Nil district. Badrawi won a seat in the assembly and occupied it for a five-year term, during which he headed the Parliamentary Committee on Education and Scientific Research. Touted as a "reformist," Badrawi also became a member of the notorious Policies Committee, drawn up and headed by the younger Mubarak.

Badrawi launched several education initiatives, both within the party and in parliament, aimed at improving Egypt's educational system. He introduced an extensive reform program for both the high school and university levels, producing numerous policy papers on dozens of education-related issues.

Badrawi also chaired a joint parliamentary committee devoted to intellectual property rights legislation, in which he pushed for the implementation of laws seen as vital to Egypt's entry into trade agreements with the European Union.

He also became a member of the state-appointed National Council for Human Rights, formed in 2004 as part of the Mubarak regime's alleged efforts to promote "democratic reform." Until 2007, he headed up the council's Committee on Social Rights. Badrawi also became a member of the board of trustees of Egypt's high-profile library, the Bibliotheca Alexandrina.

Badrawi ran again in 2005 parliamentary polls, but lost his seat to businessman Hisham Mostafa Khalil, son of a former prime minister and NDP founder. Badrawi later accused the ruling party's "old guard" of supporting Khalil's parliamentary bid at the expense of his own.

Before the Revolution

After failing to win a parliamentary seat in 2005, Badrawi launched a scathing attack against old guard figures, whom he accused of doing "everything possible" to prevent him from winning a seat in the assembly. He also accused them of conspiring to thwart his ascendance within party ranks.

Some contend that old guard officials, for their part, had always viewed Badrawi as member of Gamal Mubarak's inner circle, which they believed had been created to challenge their long-entrenched influence within the party.

Opposition forces, meanwhile, saw Badrawi largely as a tool of the younger Mubarak, used to impose the latter's liberal agenda and advance a suspected father-to-son succession scenario. Badrawi was widely quoted as saying at the time: "If President Hosni Mubarak doesn't stand in 2011 elections, it's natural that the NDP select Gamal Mubarak as its [presidential] candidate."

In September 2010, Badrawi attacked the opposition for its criticism of Gamal Mubarak's visit to Washington on what was rumored to be "semi-official" visit aimed at obtaining US approval of Gamal's plans for a presidential bid in 2011.

When Badrawi was unseated in 2005 polls, Gamal Mubarak appointed him to the chairmanship of the NDP's business committee. Gamal also pushed his aging father to appoint Badrawi to the Shura Council—the upper, consultative house of Egypt's parliament—in 2007.

The Revolution and Beyond

When faced with Egypt's popular uprising in January, longstanding president Hosni Mubarak hastily attempted to polish the image of his autocratic NDP by appointing officials seen as more amenable to the public. Badrawi found himself at the top of the list.

On 5 February 2011, only six days before Mubarak's departure, leading NDP members were forced to resign their positions en masse. At that point, Badrawi replaced NDP stalwart Safwat El-Sherif as the party's secretary general. Badrawi was also made head of the party's influential Policies Committee, replacing Gamal Mubarak, who until then had been widely perceived as the party's heir-apparent for the presidency.

In his first public statement following his appointment, Badrawi, hinting at the possibility of early presidential elections, asserted that Egyptian politics required a "new generation" and a "genuine program of radical reform."

As the popular uprising gathered momentum following international appeals for Mubarak to step down, Badrawi called on the president to hand over executive authority to his newly appointed vice president, former intelligence chief Omar Suleiman, rather than simply leave office. Such a move, Badrawi argued at the time, would pave the way for free presidential elections. "Egypt isn't in need of tragic developments that don't allow for economic development," he said. "We want work. We want companies to make profits and pay taxes. We want safety and stability."

During the crucial days of 9 and 10 February 2011, Badrawi made several visits to the presidential palace. He claims he was trying to convince Mubarak to parley with young revolutionary representatives. "This might have convinced these young people that Mubarak had already discarded the [presidential] inheritance scenario and embarked on a true democratic agenda," Badrawi later stated. "And in return, revolutionaries might have put an end to their ongoing sit-in in Tahrir Square."

Badrawi subsequently noted that Gamal Mubarak, First Lady Suzanne Mubarak, and Presidential Chief-of-Staff Zakaria Azmi all opposed efforts to open dialogue with the young revolutionaries.

As a result, Badrawi said on 10 February that: "I met President Mubarak [on 9 February] and told him that it was time to delegate his powers to Suleiman, and I expect he will do this tonight." He also later said that, on 9 February, he had urged the president by phone to brief the public about his intentions. "My aim was to urge the president to entrust his vice president with staging open presidential elections under judicial supervision as soon as possible," he was later quoted as saying.

Mubarak, however, in a speech delivered late on 10 February, defied all calls for his immediate resignation, saying he would remain in office until a September vote. The president's day-to-day powers, meanwhile, would be delegated to Suleiman.

The gesture failed to placate irate protesters, however, who had been demanding the ouster of Mubarak and his regime since 25 January. It also failed to placate Badrawi, who decided to resign after only six days as NDP secretary-general. Badrawi later recalled that, "On 11 February, there was no hope," noting that "calls for Mubarak's immediate ouster had gained powerful momentum locally and internationally." At that moment, Badrawi said, "it became clear to me that it would be better to quit the NDP before Mubarak resigned and the party collapsed into pieces."

After Mubarak finally stepped down and conditions for establishing political parties were dramatically eased, Badrawi decided to reenter domestic politics. There were reports circulating immediately after his resignation from the NDP that he attempted to form a party by the name of the Youth of January 25, but such a party never came to surface. Instead, he joined several intellectuals and businessmen to form the Ittihad (Union) Party, and is also widely believed to have played a central role in the establishment of the Misr Al-Nahda (Egypt Renaissance) Party, formed by former young cadres of the now-defunct NDP. Both parties claim to stand for political and economic liberalization.

In August 2011, Badrawi attempted to make a popular comeback with an appearance on popular television talk show *Akher Kalam*, during which he spoke about his role in the final days of the Mubarak regime. On live television, he asserted that he had personally asked the embattled president to step down at the height of the uprising and stressed his sympathy for the protesters and their demands.

His television appearance, however, was not well received by the public. Although many political observers continue to express fears of a concerted, counter-revolutionary effort to return NDP stalwarts to Egypt's political scene, Badrawi says he is simply a founder of the nascent Ittihad Party.

Mohamed Al-Beltagy

Born in 1963, Mohamed Ibrahim Al-Beltagy is a leading member of Egypt's influential Muslim Brotherhood (MB) movement and the Cairo secretary general of the Freedom and Justice Party, the MB's political arm. A medical doctor by profession, Al-Beltagy served as a Brotherhood Member of Parliament from 2005 to 2010. During his tenure as an MP, he forcefully challenged the government's performance on numerous issues, including a controversial ferryboat accident, the bird and swine flu, real estate taxes, and skyrocketing inflation.

Before the Revolution

As a teenager, Al-Beltagy explored Egypt's multifarious political trends, attending events held by different parties and groups, including those of left-wing and liberal orientation. At the age of sixteen, he decided to join the MB.

"I joined the Brotherhood because I felt it was a project that could contribute to the development of the countries of the region after years of decay," Al-Beltagy has been quoted as saying.

Ever since, he has worked on establishing MB groups throughout faculties and branches of Al-Azhar University. Al-Beltagy studied medicine at Al-Azhar University's Alexandria branch, where he was a leading figure in student union politics. Along with pursuing student activism, he excelled academically until he graduated with a degree in medicine in 1988. Following graduation, he was denied a position at the university due to his political activities, although he was given a position four years later following a court order to this effect.

His first political role came after his successful election to parliament in Egypt's 2005 legislative elections. As the MB captured an unprecedented one-fifth of the assembly, Al-Beltagy succeeded in winning a seat in parliament for Cairo's Shubra Al Khcima district. For the next five years, he served as a leading figure in the MB's parliamentary bloc, which had the distinction of being the largest opposition bloc in the People's Assembly.

In parliament, his stances on various issues—especially education—brought him to prominence. Al-Beltagy has since served as the MB's representative in a number of political initiatives, including the National Association for Change, reform campaign, and Gaza-bound aid flotillas. Al-Beltagy has also expressed his openness to dialogue with other political trends and international players.

Al-Beltagy ran for re-election in the 2010 parliamentary races. He withdrew from runoff elections, however, following an MB decision to pull out of the contest altogether due to widespread reports of electoral fraud by Mubarak's ruling National Democratic Party.

The Revolution and Beyond

Al-Beltagy participated in Egypt's January 25 Revolution from its very first day —25 January—despite an initial decision by the MB leadership not to officially endorse the uprising. Throughout the course of the eighteen-day uprising, Al-Beltagy was an active participant in the historical events taking place in Cairo's Tahrir Square.

Four months later, he took part—again, on an individual basis—in the 27 May 2011 demonstrations (dubbed the "Second Revolution of Rage"), despite a decision by MB leaders to refrain from participating.

He won a seat in the 2011/2012 parliamentary elections, and served in the 2012 People's Assembly, the parliament's lower house, until it was dissolved by court order in June 2012.

Yasser Borhami

Yasser Hussein Borhami is a prominent Salafist preacher and deputy leader of Al-Daawa Movement (*Al-Da'wa Al-Salafiyya*), a Salafist movement that spawned Al-Nour Party in 2011. Borhami was born in 1958 in Kafr Al-Dawar in the northern governorate of Beheira, and his father, a member of the Muslim Brotherhood (MB), was imprisoned under Nasser in 1965.

Borhami graduated from Alexandria University with a degree in medicine in 1982 and earned a master's degree in pediatrics in 1992. He went on to obtain a degree in Sharia from Al-Azhar University in 1999. Borhami authored several books on religion such as, *No God but Allah is the Saving Word.*

As a university student, Borhami was active in Salafist circles, and was affiliated with Al-Gamaa Al-Islamiyya (the Islamic Group). While on pilgrimage in Mecca during his second year of college, Borhami met the late Abdel Aziz bin Baz, a prominent Saudi Islamic scholar, who greatly influenced Borhami's thinking about religion.

Many Salafist figures were arrested in 1980 during President Anwar Sadat's crackdown against major opposition forces, and their absence from the scene catapulted Borhami into the public sphere. In 1987, he was detained for a month in connection with the attempt on the life of Interior Minister Hassan Abu Basha.

Before the Revolution

Before the January 25 Revolution, Borhami was a prominent preacher and key figure in Al-Daawa Movement. Al-Daawa was founded in 1984. The state disbanded the movement in 1994, and many of its key members were arrested.

Borhami is often hailed as a prominent scholar of puritan Islam. However, he was criticized for his attempts to calm down public uproar over the death of Salafist activist Sayed Belal in the custody of State Security Investigations Services in early January 2011. Belal, who was arrested in connection with a church bombing in Alexandria in December 2010, was reportedly tortured to death while in police custody. While non-Islamist groups like April 6 movement blamed Egyptian authorities for Belal's death and called for punishing those responsible, Borhami, to the disappointment of disgruntled Salafist activists, asked followers to "be patient" and exercise restraint.

The Revolution and Beyond

When asked if it was sinful to participate in the protests called for on 25 January 2011, Borhami said that participation was not a religious sin, but that Muslims were advised not to participate.

Although Borhami discouraged political participation before Mubarak's ouster, he was instrumental in forming Al-Nour Party in 2011, commonly viewed today as Al-Daawa's political arm. In justifying the shift in his position, Borhami said, "Islam must become involved of all aspects of life, even the political, and the Islamic movement must unite."

In July 2011, Borhami supported a SCAF-issued statement calling for a halt to public demonstrations so as to avoid chaos and instability.

Borhami supported Al-Nour Party's candidates for the 2011/2012 elections, and regularly spoke at the party's campaign rallies.

Prior to the 2011 election season, Borhami held the view that women should not serve in parliament. After the inclusion of women on electoral lists became a legal requirement, however, he justified Al-Nour Party's decision to field women candidates as a necessary step to ensure that the party could win as many seats in parliament as possible. Al-Nour Party officials assured its supporters that female candidates would remain in the tail of their electoral lists and, thus, would have a very little chance of securing representation. Borhami attended and spoke at Al-Nour's first women conference, which the party organized to enhance its outreach to female supporters and potential supporters. The party's detractors, however, cynically mocked this initiative, pointing out that none of the speakers at the event were women, but rather a handful of old men lecturing female attendees about the nature and scope of their political rights.

ZIAD AL-ELEIMI

Ziad Al-Eleimi is a founding member of the Egyptian Social Democratic Party, and served in the People's Assembly in 2012 before it was dissolved by court order in June 2012. He is also a lawyer, human rights activist, founding, and leading member of the now-dissolved Revolution's Youth Coalition (RYC). The RYC was a loosely affiliated group of youth-oriented opposition movements that emerged during the eighteen-day uprising that toppled former president Hosni Mubarak. It was dissolved in July 2012.

Before the Revolution

Al-Eleimi's involvement in politics began early in his life, being the son of Ekram Yousef, a prominent student activist in the politically turbulent 1970s. Thus, by his teenage years Al-Eleimi was already involved in social and political struggle.

During his law school years, Al-Eleimi was closely engaged in student activism and joined the Egyptian Popular Committee in Solidarity with the Palestinian Intifada, an Egyptian movement formed in 2000 in solidarity with the second Palestinian Intifada.

After graduating in 2002, Al-Eleimi started his own law practice, cooperating with NGOs involved in fighting human rights abuses and sexual harassment, including Al-Nadeem Center, the Hisham Mubarak Law Center, and the New Woman Foundation.

Al-Eleimi moved into the spotlight as a leading member of Mohamed ElBaradei's National Association for Change, which sought to gather public support for democratic reforms in 2010. Al-Eleimi was often seen by the side of ElBaradei, the former IAEA chief who offered himself as a potential alternative to then-incumbent president Hosni Mubarak. After the January 25 Revolution, Al-Eleimi became active in newly formed parties and movements.

Before the revolution, Al-Eleimi was one of the leading figures involved in Al-Bosla, a group formed in 2005 with the goal of shaping emerging democratic liberation movements in Egypt. Al-Eleimi, along with other members of Al-Bosla, joined the Egyptian Social Democratic Party since its creation in 2011, one of the country's most influential left-of-center parties.

Al-Eleimi was one of many who organized the 25 January protests, not knowing at the time that they would ultimately lead to the downfall of the Mubarak regime. Before that, Al-Eleimi was active in organizing protests against police brutality and sectarian strife.

The Revolution and Beyond

As a leading member of the now-dissolved Revolution's Youth Coalition (RYC), Al-Eleimi was closely engaged with organizing protests during the January 25 Revolution.

The RYC was formed during the early stages of last winter's eighteen-day uprising and included representatives of the ElBaradei Campaign for Change, the April 6 movement, the Democratic Front Youth, the Muslim Brotherhood Youth, and others. It was dissolved in July 2012 after the beginning of the Mohamed Morsi presidency.

In addition to being one of its leading members, Al-Eleimi was the RYC's official spokesperson. The RYC's first slogan was "no turning back before Mubarak's departure." The alliance set up camp in Tahrir Square, continuing to coordinate the sit-in until Mubarak's resignation was announced on 11 February 2011.

Even after Mubarak's ouster, the RYC remained vocal on political issues and continued to participate in major demonstrations and sit-ins. Al-Eleimi's lengthy involvement in the RYC speaks to his belief in the power of "street politics."

Al-Eleimi was an outspoken critic of the Supreme Council of the Armed Forces (SCAF). The RYC had announced in April 2011 that it would suspend dialogue with SCAF following a violent crackdown by the army on Tahrir Square protesters that same month.

While Revolution's Youth Coalition was a member of the Revolution Continues electoral coalition, as a member of the Egyptian Social Democratic Party, Al-Eleimi contested the 2011/2012 parliamentary elections through the Egyptian Bloc, a rival electoral coalition. Al-Eleimi ran on the top of the Bloc's list in South Cairo's district of Al-Moqattam, where he participated in social work for the past four years. He was elected to serve in the People's Assembly, the parliament's lower house, which was dissolved by court order in June 2012.

Amr Hamzawy

Born in 1968, Amr Hamzawy is an Egyptian political scientist, activist, and a member of the 2012 People's Assembly, which was dissolved by court order in June 2012. He is the founder of the liberal Egypt Freedom Party, established in the aftermath of Egypt's January 25 Revolution.

Until February 2011, Hamzawy was a senior associate at the Carnegie Endowment for International Peace, serving as research director at the organization's Beirut office. His research focuses on issues of political reform and political Islamist movements in the Middle East. Hamzawy's profile in the Arab world rose in 2006, when he became a frequent political commentator on pan-Arab media outlets, including influential satellite news network Al Jazeera.

He currently teaches political science at Cairo University and the American University in Cairo. Hamzawy received his PhD from the Free University of Berlin.

Before the Revolution

Before the revolution, Hamzawy was known for his research and analytical writings that examined the role of Islamist political movements within the context of democratic change in the region.

In 2007, Hamzawy co-authored a Carnegie paper criticizing the constitutional amendments proposed in 2006 by Mubarak with the stated aim of "liberalizing" Egypt's political system. Hamzawy and his co-authors contended that the amendments would effectively serve to limit political freedoms while misleadingly conveying the appearance of liberalization.

A few weeks later, Egyptian state-owned media launched a media campaign against Hamzawy. One state-owned newspaper claimed that Hamzawy had played a role in opening channels of communication between the Muslim Brotherhood (MB) and the US government. Hamzawy denied the allegations in a written statement, which was later republished on the MB's official English website.

According to Mustafa Al-Fiqi, a former aide to Mubarak, Hamzawy was previously affiliated with Mubarak's now-defunct National Democratic Party (NDP). He only left the ruling party, Al-Fiqi said, after it became clear that he would not be able to rise up in the party's ranks. Hamzawy insists, however, that the extent of his involvement in the NDP was his attendance at a few meetings of the "Egypt and World Committee" in 2003. Hamzawy said he found the meetings pointless and thus decided to drop out.

Hamzawy was also a vocal critic of apparent efforts by the former regime to groom Mubarak's influential son, Gamal Mubarak, to succeed his father as president. In a 2008 interview, Hamzawy described the younger Mubarak as "lacking legitimacy."

A few days before the eruption of the January 25 Revolution, Hamzawy told a BBC interviewer that the Tunisian revolution would not be replicated in Egypt, since the circumstances of the Tunisian middle class, which spearheaded the uprising, were completely different from those of their Egyptian counterparts.

The Revolution and Beyond

During the eighteen-day uprising that ultimately toppled Mubarak, Hamzawy became the spokesman for the "Committee of Wise Men" set up during the revolution to mediate between anti-Mubarak demonstrators and the regime. News reports state that Hamzawy had been offered the post of youth minister in the Ahmed Shafik government, but that he declined it.

As a Washington-based researcher, Hamzawy's work served to refute Western misconceptions about Islamist movements in the Arab world and their stated commitment to democratic change. Ironically, as he took a more active role in Egyptian politics after the revolution, his liberal orientation put him on a collision course with local Islamist groups.

In a famous debate at the American University in Cairo in the spring of 2011, Hamzawy got into a heated argument with MB spokesperson Essam Al-Eryan on the legitimacy of the SCAF-proposed constitutional amendments, which Hamzawy opposed. During the debate, Hamzawy accused Al-Eryan of adopting the same condescending approach that the Mubarak regime had used in its dialogue with the opposition.

Hamzawy also came under attack from the Islamic Group (Al-Gamaa Al-Islamiyya), whose leader, Nageh Ibrahim, accused Hamzawy of collaborating with Mubarak's NDP and the US government. Ibrahim also asserted that Hamzawy had opportunistically jumped on the revolutionary bandwagon, while having made no previous contributions to Egyptian politics.

Hamzawy participated in the founding of the Egyptian Social Democratic Party, but later left it to protest a party statement issued in condemnation of the military's use of violence against Tahrir Square demonstrators on 9 April 2011. Hamzawy complained that the party had failed to consult him in the drafting of the statement.

In the aftermath of the incident, Hamzawy said he rejected attempts to instigate conflict between the army and people during Egypt's critical transitional phase. Six months later, Hamzawy stated that the country's military leaders were no longer impartial arbiters in Egypt's ongoing political battles, but rather a bona fide party to the conflicts in question.

Hamzawy currently heads up the Egypt Freedom Party. The party had briefly been a member of the Democratic Alliance, a MB-led electoral coalition, but withdrew in early August 2011. The party later stated that it had pulled out of the alliance because alliance members had seemed unserious about developing consensus among its constituent organizations regarding the principles that would ultimately guide efforts to draw up a new constitution.

The Egypt Freedom Party was subsequently involved in the Egyptian Bloc, a rival electoral coalition founded by secular-leaning parties. But, once again, Hamzawy's party withdrew from the bloc, citing a lack of transparency in the candidate selection process and concerns that some coalition members were fielding candidates once affiliated with Mubarak's dismantled NDP.

In the 2011/2012 parliamentary polls, the Egypt Freedom Party fielded twenty-two candidates, including Hamzawy, through the Revolution Continues electoral coalition, which comprised an ideologically diverse set of political actors, including liberals, Islamists, and socialists.

In the run-up to Egypt's fraught electoral season, Hamzawy emerged as a strong advocate for the adoption of a party list electoral system, and a critic of SCAF's insistence on allocating a proportion of parliamentary seats based on individual candidacy electoral contests. In the end, however, he decided to run in an individual candidacy parliamentary race in the Cairo district of Heliopolis. Hamzawy claims he did not run on a party list himself because he wanted to make room for young candidates to run on the Revolution Continues list. Hamzawy ran against Egyptian Current Party leader Asmaa Mahfouz, even though both were members of the same electoral coalition. Hamzawy won the seat and served in the 2012 parliament until it was dissolved by court order in June 2012.

OSAMA AL-GHAZALI HARB

A veteran politician, Osama Al-Ghazali Harb, born in 1947, is the head and the one of the founders of Egypt's liberal-leaning Democratic Front Party.

After graduating from Cairo University's Faculty of Economics and Political Science in 1969, he began his journalistic career working for the state-owned *Al-Gomhorriya* newspaper and *Al-Kateb* magazine. In 1977, he moved to the Ahram Center for Political and Strategic Studies to work as a researcher and in 1990 replaced Boutros-Boutros Ghali as editor-in-chief of *International Politics* magazine (*Al-Siyasa Al-Dawliyya*), one of the center's most prestigious publications. His work with the center officially ended in 2010 after its administration refused to renew his contract.

Before the Revolution

As a student, Harb was a member of the Socialist Youth Organization since its establishment in 1965. The organization was affiliated with the Arab Socialist Union, officially the ruling party in Egypt between 1962 and 1978. In 1972, he was arrested on charges of belonging to an organization (the Arab Pioneers) "that seeks to overthrow the regime." As a result, his mandatory military service was terminated.

He was again arrested in 1975 as a member of the Communist Party, during a wave of arrests that targeted leftist and socialist forces. His third arrest came during Cairo's 1977 Bread Riots. He was released in the late 1970s after which he focused on his academic career until 1995, when then-president Hosni Mubarak first appointed him as a member of Egypt's Shura Council, the upper house of parliament.

In 2002, he was appointed to the notorious Policies Committee of the now dissolved National Democratic Party (NDP) of ousted president Hosni Mubarak, which stood behind Egypt's drive towards economic liberalization and privatization during the last decade. However, he resigned from the Policies Committee in 2006, allegedly because he objected to the NDP-sponsored amendment of Article 76 of the constitution. The amendment reinforced the NDP's monopoly over political power by making it difficult for competitive opposition candidates to get their name on the presidential election ballot.

In 2007, Harb joined forces with Yehia Al-Gamal to establish the Democratic Front Party, initially called the Justice and Freedom Party. The party adopts a liberal orientation, calling for a civil state and a free—if regulated—market. Later the same year, he was elected party chair.

In 2010, the Democratic Front Party became one of the major supporters of

Mohamed ElBaradei's call for far reaching democratic reforms, including an open presidential election in which candidates that were not handpicked by the Mubarak regime could run.

The Revolution and Beyond

Harb's Democratic Front Party supported Egypt's January 25 Revolution from the outset, issuing a statement on 2 February 2011 demanding Mubarak's departure and the temporary transfer of executive authority to Egypt's acting vice president.

His party was among the political forces that rejected a raft of amendments to the 1971 constitution that was put up for approval in a national referendum in March 2011. At the time, Harb argued that the amendments would only serve to lend legitimacy to the now-defunct constitution.

Harb was a staunch supporter of drafting a new constitution in advance of holding elections, even going so far as to endorse the idea that the ruling Supreme Council of the Armed Forces (SCAF) remain in power for at least two more years to accomplish this end. Harb argued, "the security presence is very weak and we still need extra time to reshuffle the police force, which was completely destroyed during the revolution." Many activists, like Al-Wasat's Essam Sultan, criticized Harb's comments, viewing them as an implicit endorsement of extended military rule. Interestingly, a month later Harb blamed the delay in ending military rule on the Muslim Brotherhood, specifically for the group's insistence on holding elections before drafting a new national charter.

Harb has also defended SCAF's "delay" in issuing a law banning former NDP members from contesting elections, arguing that "the NDP had a lot of respectable figures" and noting that it would take considerable time to determine which members of the former ruling party were corrupt and which ones were not.

Harb was scheduled to head a SCAF-appointed committee tasked with drafting a set of principles that would guide constitution-writing efforts after parliamentary elections. However, he later announced on 15 July 2011 that the SCAF had cancelled his mandate and aborted the idea all together.

When electoral alliances began to crystallize in the run-up to polling, Harb joined forces with the MB's Freedom and Justice Party and Al-Wafd Party, among others, to create the Democratic Alliance for Egypt. His party eventually withdrew from the electoral coalition on grounds that a partnership with Islamist groups is inconsistent with the party's liberal principles. Party officials, however, did not explain why they joined an alliance that clashed with their party's principles in the first place. The Democratic Front later helped form the Egyptian Bloc, a secular leaning electoral alliance that was widely viewed as a counterbalance to the MB. The party eventually withdrew from the bloc and chose to contest elections independently from any coalitions.

Harb has never before contested parliamentary elections, with his seat in the Shura Council having come via presidential appointment. Harb did not contest Egypt's 2011 legislative elections.

Amin Iskandar

Amin Iskandar is a founding member of Al-Karama (Dignity) Party and is known for his nationalist and Nasserist leanings. Born in 1952, Iskandar is a writer and researcher and published a number of writings on Egyptian and Arab politics.

Before the Revolution

Iskandar was formerly a member of the Nasserist Party, but his membership was frozen in 1998 after he, along with other members of his generation, fell out with the party's leaders. Although the party leadership had been willing to allow Iskandar and his fellows back into the party's ranks, they declined and instead established their own political party, Al-Karama.

When they applied for a party license from the state-controlled Political Parties Committee, however, the request was refused outright. The party only managed to obtain official recognition following the January 25 Revolution that unseated longstanding president Hosni Mubarak. Al-Karama Party was officially approved on 29 August 2011.

Iskandar began his political activism as an avowed Nasserist as part of Egypt's student movement in the 1970s, winning student union elections twice. He was arrested during the 1977 Bread Riots. He was also arrested during Egypt's parliamentary races in the 1980s and in 1983, when he was accused of belonging to an armed underground Nasserist organization. While in prison, Iskandar was severely tortured.

In 2000, Iskandar played an important role in the Egyptian solidarity movement with the Palestinian Intifada and the wave of popular protests against the 2003 US-led invasion and occupation of Iraq. He is one of the main founders of the Kefaya protest movement. Iskandar became known for his vocal criticism of the Mubarak regime, vociferously censuring the notion of "presidential inheritance," which is shorthand for the former regime's presumed plans to pass on the presidency to Mubarak's son, Gamal Mubarak.

The Revolution and Beyond

Iskandar was arrested on 25 January 2011—the day the revolution erupted—while demonstrating in the Cairo district of Shubra, where he resides. After being released two days later, he became an active participant in the eighteen-day uprising that eventually culminated in Mubarak's ouster. He currently serves as secretary-general of Al-Karama Party.

In the run-up to Egypt's first post-Mubarak parliamentary polls, Al-Karama joined the Democratic Alliance's electoral coalition through which it contested the parliamentary elections. Spearheaded by the Freedom and Justice Party, the political arm of the MB, the Democratic Alliance had also briefly included the liberal Al-Wafd Party, which eventually withdrew from the coalition.

The nascent Al-Karama Party, along with a handful of other parties, came under criticism in October 2011 after it agreed to sign an eight-point proposal tabled by Egypt's ruling Supreme Council of the Armed Forces (SCAF). The proposal included a promise to amend Article 5 of the elections law to allow political parties to field candidates for the one-third of the seats in parliament previously reserved for independent nominees.

Other post-revolution political forces slammed the agreement, however, for its inclusion of an article on the longstanding emergency law. The article effectively condoned the law's application without providing an exact date for its expiration. The agreement was also criticized for including an article stating the signatories' support for SCAF and its role in managing Egypt's transitional period.

Despite these criticisms, Iskandar defended his party's decision to sign the SCAF-prepared document, arguing that the agreement had served to realize several demands that the opposition advanced, including the amendment of Article 5.

A Coptic Christian, Amin Iskandar has always championed the rights of Egypt's Coptic minority. After the violent 9 October Maspero clashes, when military personnel attacked Coptic demonstrators leaving at least twenty-six dead, Iskandar described the incident as "the most dangerous precedent ever witnessed by Egypt."

Iskandar ran in the parliamentary polls as a member of Al-Karama Party and won. He served in the People's Assembly, the parliament's lower house, until it was dissolved by court order in June 2012.

ABUL ELA MADI

Born in 1958 in the Upper Egyptian governorate of Minya, Abul Ela Madi is Al-Wasat Party's leader and one of its most prominent cofounders. He graduated in 1984 from Minya University with a degree in engineering and earned a law degree in 2008.

After defecting from Egypt's Muslim Brotherhood (MB) movement in 1996, he went on to form Al-Wasat Party, commonly known as an Islamist party with a "moderate" interpretation of Islamic divine texts. After several unsuccessful attempts to obtain a party license under the regime of ousted president Hosni Mubarak, Al-Wasat was finally recognized in the immediate wake of the January 25 Revolution.

He is also a founding member of the Misr for Dialogue and Culture, a non-profit organization devoted to Muslim-Christian dialogue.

Madi boasts a number of published works and has participated in numerous conferences devoted to the subjects of political Islam and interfaith relations.

Before the Revolution

Madi first became involved in politics during his student years, winning consecutive student union elections at Minya University from 1977 to 1979. In 1979, while in prison for his university political activism, Madi joined the MB. Beforehand, he was a member of the Islamic Group (Al-Gamaa Al-Islamiyya). In 1996, however, he split from the Brotherhood due to disagreements over political strategy. He has had a tense relationship with the MB ever since he left it.

Shortly after leaving the MB, Madi established Al-Wasat Party, based on a "moderate-Islamist" platform.

Al-Wasat's application for a party license was turned down multiple times by the state controlled Political Parties Committee, which decreed that the would-be party "did not have anything new" to add to existing party platforms.

In 1996, Madi was hauled before a military tribunal alongside other party founders for allegedly trying to form a political party as a front for an "illegal organization," namely the Muslim Brotherhood. He was released two months later.

In 2000, however, he managed to obtain a license from Egypt's Social Affairs Ministry for the establishment of a non-profit organization, Misr for Dialogue and Culture, which aims to foster Muslim-Christian dialogue.

Madi is known for his moderate interpretation of Islamic divine texts. He has repeatedly stated that Al-Wasat, unlike the MB, does not oppose the notion of a woman or non-Muslim serving as head of state. He also claims that his party boasts a number of Coptic Christians as members.

Madi is further known for his criticism of the Brotherhood's centralized decision-making style and ironclad discipline, as well as his appeals to engage with non-Islamist political forces. In 2005, he became a founding member of the Kefaya protest movement, which brought together an ideologically diverse set of opposition actors, including Islamists, liberals, leftists, and nationalists. Kefaya was the first opposition movement to demand that Mubarak step down as Egypt's president.

He also repeatedly called for less confrontational tactics vis-à-vis the state. For example, in a 2000 *Ahram Weekly* interview, he criticized the MB for escalating tensions between Islamists and the state by being too confrontational and insisting on contesting elections. In the same interview, Madi stated his support for "competent candidates," including some fielded by Mubarak's ruling National Democratic Party.

Madi has considered the long fight for official recognition of the Al-Wasat Party as a new strategy espousing a more public and legal form of political dissent, in contrast to the MB's underground activism.

The Revolution and Beyond

Madi, along with members of Al-Wasat Party, supported Egypt's January 25 Revolution from the outset. In an apparent attempt to highlight its revolutionary credentials, Al-Wasat adopted "From Tahrir Square to Parliament" as its campaign slogan for the 2011/2012 parliamentary elections. Following Mubarak's ouster, Madi has repeatedly stated that the trials of the deposed president should serve as a "warning to any future leader or president."

Madi also defended the raft of constitutional amendments proposed by a committee appointed by Egypt's ruling Supreme Council of the Armed Forces (SCAF) in the revolution's wake. His party, meanwhile, zealously campaigned for the amendments, which were ultimately endorsed by seventy-seven percent of those who voted in a nationwide referendum in March 2011.

Liberal and leftist activists opposed these amendments on the grounds that they failed to overhaul the "authoritarian constitution" inherited from the Mubarak era, whereas Al-Wasat's leaders, along with other Islamist groups, claimed that approving these amendments was the best way to ensure a swift end to military rule.

Since the uprising, Al-Wasat Party has advocated for a speedy transition to an elected government. It has opposed several of the post-revolution Tahrir Square sit-ins in 2011, arguing that elections should remain the public's primary focus.

Madi has also opposed an official initiative by Al-Azhar scholars to build greater consensus among Egypt's diverse political forces, particularly around the principles to guide the writing of the country's next constitution. He has argued that Al-Azhar should refrain from interfering in politics and should focus exclusively on religious affairs. "If Al-Azhar is allowed to enter politics, then so should the Pope," he was quoted as saying.

Madi ran in the 2011/2012 parliamentary elections. Al-Wasat's list in Minya, headed by Madi, entered into a competitive race against the Freedom and Justice list headed by Saad Al-Katatny. Al-Katatny is the Secretary General of the Freedom and Justice Party, founded by the Brotherhood, the same group from which Madi defected in the mid-1990s. Ultimately, Madi lost the race, and Al-Katatny won and became the speaker of the lower house of parliament.

Al-Wasat Party participated in the parliamentary elections without being part of any formal electoral coalition. The party was briefly part of the Muslim Brotherhood-led Democratic Alliance for Egypt, but withdrew due to what party leaders described as the Muslim Brotherhood's domineering role in the alliance.

Madi boasts considerable electoral experience. Along with winning student union elections during his Minya University career, he was also elected assistant secretary general of the Egyptian Engineer's Syndicate, a post that he held from 1987 to 1995.

In 1987, while still with the MB, Madi was nominated to run in parliamentary elections, but his candidacy was dropped due to a law stipulating that an individual had to be at least thirty years old to run for office. Madi was twenty-nine at the time.

Madi went on to run in the 1995 parliamentary polls as an MB candidate in Cairo's Helwan district, but lost. His decision to split from the MB later the same year drew the ire of that group's leadership.

MUSTAFA AL-NAGGAR

Mustafa Al-Naggar is former general coordinator of the campaign supporting presidential hopeful Mohamed ElBaradei. After the January 25 Revolution, he helped form Al-Adl Party.

Al-Naggar also ran the popular blog, "I am with them," and, since 2007, has been actively blogging about human rights and civil liberties in Egypt.

Born in Alexandria in 1980, Mustafa Al-Naggar has a bachelor's degree in dentistry and mass communication from Cairo University and the American University in Cairo (AUC), respectively.

Al-Naggar hails from a family sympathetic to Egypt's Muslim Brotherhood (MB) movement, and his grandfather, Kamal Abdel Tawab, was a leading MB figure. Al-Naggar himself became a member of the MB's youth wing, although he eventually left it in 2005.

"After 2005 parliamentary polls, in which the MB won eighty-eight seats in the People's Assembly, I withdrew from the group because I no longer identified with its platform and ideology," Al-Naggar told *Jadaliyya/Ahram Online*.

Since then, he has embraced a more "centrist" approach to Egyptian politics that would eventually become the basis for his Al-Adl Party.

Before the Revolution

Al-Naggar has played an active role in Mohamed ElBaradei's National Association for Change (NAC) reform movement. The association is a coalition of opposition figures and groups formed in 2010 to demand democratic reforms as well as free and fair presidential election in which independent candidates that were not handpicked by the Mubarak regime could run.

Al-Naggar's online human rights advocacy earned him an honorary award from the UNHCR in Beirut in 2010. He also served as coordinator for the Arab Journalists and Bloggers Network for Human Rights.

The Revolution and Beyond

Al-Naggar actively participated in Egypt's January 25 Revolution and was present for the eighteen-day Tahrir Square sit-in that ultimately led to Mubarak's ouster. He was among the first of the young revolutionaries to call on the Egyptian people to focus on parliamentary elections with a view to preparing the public for the looming electoral contests.

He went on to co-found Al-Adl (Justice) Party, which seeks to carve for itself a centrist position in Egypt's post-revolution political landscape away from the ideological spats dividing secular and Islamist trends. Al-Adl Party claims it does not adhere to any particular ideology and has tried unsuccessfully to forge an electoral alliance called the "Third Way."

Al-Naggar stirred controversy within Al-Adl after he agreed to a highly contentious statement prepared by the ruling military council, along with thirteen other parties. The document implicitly upheld the extension of Egypt's emergency law, although it offered parties some concessions related to election laws. Al-Naggar subsequently retracted his endorsement of the statement.

Although the 2011/2012 elections was the first time for Al-Naggar to run in parliamentary polls, he is no stranger to electoral campaigning, since he served as coordinator for ElBaradei's presidential campaign. Al-Naggar ran in Cairo's Nasr City district for an individual seat on behalf of Al-Adl. After winning the race, he served in the People's Assembly, the parliament's lower house, until it was dissolved by court order in June 2012.

Mohamed Al-Qasas

A former member of the influential Muslim Brotherhood (MB), Mohamed Al-Qasas is one of the main founders of the Egyptian Current Party (Al-Tayyar Al-Masry). He is widely known for his prominent role within the MB's youth wing, of which he was a leading member. After the revolution, Al-Qasas was one of the MB's first activists to defy its leadership's decision to forbid members from joining any political party other than the recently licensed Freedom and Justice Party (FJP).

Born in 1974, Mohamed Al-Qasas graduated from Al-Azhar University with a degree in Arabic and Islamic studies. He works in the field of media production and manages his own production house.

Al-Qasas was a member of the now-dissolved Revolution's Youth Coalition (RYC), which he entered initially as a representative of the MB youth wing. The MB later expelled him for co-founding and joining the Egyptian Current Party in defiance of the Brotherhood's leadership. Al-Qasas, along with several other young MB-affiliated RYC members, also disobeyed MB leadership directives when they supported the RYC's decision to take part in mass demonstrations on 27 May, dubbed the "Second Revolution of Rage." Shortly afterward, the MB officially stated that it had "no representatives" in the RYC.

Al-Qasas, along with other young MB members and several former and current affiliates of the April 6 youth movement, joined forces to establish the Egyptian Current Party. The party holds that Islam is only one element of a multiplicity of cultural identities that constitute contemporary Egyptian society.

Even before his expulsion from the MB, Al-Qasas had been a prominent supporter of greater dialogue between the country's diverse political and ideological trends. As an MB member he was an advocate of increased cooperation between the group and non-Islamist political movements. He also played an important role in coordinating joint MB, nationalist, and leftist efforts.

Before the Revolution

Prior to the January 25 Revolution, Al-Qasas had been a leading member of the MB's youth wing. He was politically active as a student at Cairo University, where he took part in demonstrations and marches. These varied from supporting the Palestinian national cause, opposing the US-led wars on Iraq and Afghanistan as well as the trepidations of the Mubarak regime, and finally supporting civil rights and freedoms in Egypt.

Under the Mubarak regime, Al-Qasas was arrested four times for his political activism. Authorities first arrested him, along with other MB-affiliated students, in 1999 at Cairo University to prevent them from organizing anti-Mubarak protests in the run-up to a national presidential referendum. He was again arrested in 2001 for demonstrating in solidarity with the Palestinian cause, after which he was detained for nine months together with twenty-two other MB members. Although Al-Qasas was later released, several of his colleagues received three to five year prison sentences.

He was arrested again in 2006 for demonstrating in solidarity with Egypt's independent judiciary movement. A year later, he was arrested a fourth time in conjunction with the MB's opposition to constitutional amendments introduced by the Mubarak regime with a view to facilitate the transfer of presidential authority to the president's son, Gamal.

The Revolution and Beyond

Al-Qasas was an active participant in the January 25 Revolution since its outset. He was one of the main figures within the MB's youth wing who insisted on taking part in the burgeoning protests and encouraged other young MB members to participate in defiance of their leadership's official decision not to take part.

The MB's youth wing played a vital role in the eighteen-day uprising that culminated in Mubarak's ouster. Due to their enviable levels of organization and discipline, young MB members distinguished themselves by protecting Tahrir Square protesters from Mubarak loyalists' attacks.

During the course of the revolution, Al-Qasas became a member of the RYC. The RYC was a loosely affiliated group of youth-oriented opposition movements that emerged during the eighteen-day uprising that toppled former president Hosni Mubarak. It was dissolved in July 2012.

After Mubarak's ouster, Al-Qasas violated the MB leadership's decision not to participate in mass protests calling for the implementation of key revolutionary demands. In the "Second Revolution of Rage" on 27 May 2011, Al-Qasas, along with other MB-affiliated RYC members, insisted on taking part in the protest despite the MB leadership's unwavering stance to boycott.

The following day, the MB leadership declared that it had "no representatives" in the RYC. Less than two months later, Al-Qasas, along with several colleagues, was formally expelled from the MB.

According to the MB leadership, the young activists were expelled for taking part in the establishment of the Egyptian Current Party in defiance of group directives. Some former MB members, however, say the real reasons for the expulsions were more complex, noting that those expelled also included supporters of Abdel Moneim Abul Fottoh. Abul Fottoh was a leading MB member who resigned from the group shortly after the revolution. He ran in the 2012 presidential election and lost.

The MB participated in 2010 parliamentary polls, which were reportedly rigged in favor of Mubarak's ruling party, but withdrew from the second round after winning only one seat. At the time, the MB's youth wing, in which Al-Qasas had been a leading member, played a major role in the group's electoral campaigning.

Now a leading member of the Egyptian Current Party, Al-Qasas ran in the parliamentary elections, but lost. He contested a seat in Cairo's Heliopolis district through the party list of The Revolution Continues, an electoral coalition that included the Egyptian Current Party along with the RYC, the Socialist Popular Alliance, the Egypt Freedom Party, the Equality and Development Party, and the Egyptian Alliance Party.

Naguib Sawiris

The eldest of three prominent Coptic Christian brothers, Naguib Sawiris first began investing in Egypt's nascent telecom industry in the early 1990s. This strategy soon made him the first billionaire in his family. The telecom magnate joined family-owned Orascom in 1979. Sawiris has continuously contributed to the growth of the firm, which today represents one of Egypt's largest and most diversified conglomerates. Orascom Telecom has since expanded its operations into Algeria, Tunisia, Pakistan, Bangladesh, Iraq, and North Korea.

On the 2006 Forbes list of the world's richest people, Sawiris was ranked at no. 278. He subsequently rose to number sixty-two in 2007 and number sixty in 2008. With the onset of the global economic crisis in 2009, his total wealth dropped to three billion dollars, causing his ranking on the world's billionaires list to fall to number 196.

Before the Revolution

Sawiris did not hold any political posts before Egypt's January 25 Revolution. Though known to be close to powerful political figures, he was never a member of the National Democratic Party of ousted president Hosni Mubarak, or any other bodies associated with the former regime. In 2007 and 2008, he launched the satellite television channels OTV and On-TV respectively.

Sawiris's name first came to the forefront of public discussions during the 1990s when the state awarded his company Mobinil one of two mobile telephone licenses in the country. While his political leanings were not obvious at the time, it was assumed that Sawiris enjoyed good relations with the Mubarak regime, since such licenses were usually awarded to individuals with friendly ties to the ruling party.

Some media reports assert that Sawiris was close to Mubarak's son, Gamal Mubarak, who was apparently being groomed to assume the presidency after his father. After Mubarak's downfall, however, Sawiris asserted that he had differences with Mubarak's son, but acknowledged that Mubarak's rule was not entirely negative and that his own businesses and interests have grown during the deposed president's reign.

Sawiris is also a major investor in the prominent Egyptian daily *Al-Masry Al-Youm*, which was launched in 2004 and has become one of Egypt's most widely read daily newspapers.

He was also one of the chief financiers of the Democratic Front Party, a liberal opposition party launched in 2007 and led by Osama Al-Ghazali Harb.

In 2007, some of Sawiris's comments in which he criticized the *hijab* (Islamic headscarf) sparked a heated debate. It also prompted calls from Muslim leaders to boycott Sawiris-owned companies and its products.

The Revolution and Beyond

During the revolution, Sawiris, together with a group of respected intellectuals, businessmen, and politicians, formed the Committee of Wise Men. This committee was tasked with arbitrating between the revolutionaries—in particular the Revolutionary Youth Coalition—and the Mubarak regime. While committee members claimed to support the revolution, they were also known to be closely associated with some Mubarak regime figures. Ultimately, the committee did not play a significant role in shaping the revolution's outcome.

In the wake of the revolution, Sawiris, along with a group of like-minded businessmen, established the Free Egyptians Party. Sawiris, along with the party's officials, has stated that he does not lead the Free Egyptians Party nor does he hold any official posts inside it, though media reports continue to link them.

Although Sawiris claims to stand against mixing religion and public affairs, some intellectuals have accused him of contradicting himself. In 2008, he told US interviewer Charlie Rose, "I'm a very strong believer [in Christianity] and this has always been the source of my strength–not the money."

In August 2011, Sawiris posted a link to a cartoon depicting Mickey and Minnie Mouse wearing traditional Islamic garb on his twitter account. Many Islamists perceived this picture as highly offensive and launched a massive boycott campaign against Sawiris-owned firms. The campaign adversely impacted mobile operator Mobinil, which Sawiris remains closely affiliated with but no longer owns.

4 | Laws and Processes

THE CONCISE IDIOT'S GUIDE TO THE EGYPTIAN ELECTIONS

Egypt population: 85 million total (est.)
Citizens eligible to vote: 50 million (approx.)

Parliamentary composition: bicameral, consisting of the People's Assembly (lower house) and the Shura Council (upper consultative house)

People's Assembly elections

The People's Assembly elections were conducted over three stages, each involving polling in nine governorates (out of total 27 governorates). Run-off elections were held a week later between front-runners in individual candidacy races where none of the candidates got 50%+ of the total vote.

The Assembly was elected through a mixed electoral system, whereby two-thirds of the total elected seats are chosen in accordance with a proportional representation list system. The remaining one-third was elected in accordance with an individual candidacy system.

Polling dates

The election of the People's Assembly began on 28 November 2011 and ended on 11 January 2012.

People's Assembly elections stage #1:

Polling: 28-29 November 2011; **Run-offs:** 5-6 December 2011
In: Cairo, Fayoum, Port Said, Damietta, Alexandria, Kafr El-Sheikh, Assiut, Luxor, and the Red Sea

People's Assembly elections stage #2:

Polling: 14-15 December 2011; **Run-offs**: 21-22 December 2011
In: Giza, Beni Suef, Menoufiya, Sharqiya, Ismailia, Suez, Beheira, Sohag, and Aswan

People's Assembly elections stage #3:

Polling: 3-4 January 2012; **Run-offs**: 10-11 January 2012
In: Minya, Qalyubia, Gharbiya, Daqahliyya, North Sinai, South Sinai, Marsa Matruh, Qena, and the New Valley

Note: The polling dates listed above do not take into account the unscheduled revotes that occurred in some electoral districts.

The People's Assembly: Basic Facts

People's Assembly opening session: 23 January 2012

People's Assembly total membership: 508

- Number of elected seats: 498
- Number of seats appointed by president (SCAF): 10
- Assembly seats elected via proportional representation list system: 332 from 46 constituencies
- Assembly seats elected via individual candidacy system: 166 from 83 constituencies
- Number of candidates running for People's Assembly individual candidacy seats: 6,591 competing for 166 seats
- Number of party (or party-coalition) lists competing for People's Assembly proportional representation seats: 590 lists for 332 seats

Shura Council elections

Conducted over two stages (13 governorates in the first stage and 14 in the second). Run-off elections are held a week later between front-runners in constituencies where none of the candidates got 50%+ of the total vote.

Polling dates

Shura council elections began on 29 January 2012 and ended on 22 February 2012.

Shura Council elections stage #1:

Polling: 29-30 January 2012; **Run-offs**: 7 February 2012
In: Cairo, Alexandria, Gharbiya, Daqahaliyya, Menoufiya, Damietta, North Sinai, South Sinai, Fayoum, Assiut, Qena, the Red Sea, and the New Valley

Shura Council elections stage #2:

Polling: 14-15 February 2012; **Run-offs**: 22 February 2012
In: Giza, Qalyubia, Sharqiya, Beheira, Kafr El-Sheikh, Ismailia, Port Said, Suez, Marsa Matrouh, Beni Suef, Minya, Sohag, Luxor, and Aswan

Shura Council: Basic Facts

Shura Council opening session: 28 February 2012

Shura Council total membership: 270

- Number of elected seats: 180
- Number of seats appointed by president (SCAF): 90
- Shura Council seats elected via proportional representation list system: 120 from 30 constituencies
- Shura Council seats elected via individual candidacy system: 60 from 30 constituencies
- Number of candidates running for Shura Council individual candidacy seats: 2,036 competing for 60 seats
- Number of party (or party-coalition) lists competing for Shura Council proportional representation seats: 272 lists for 120 seats

Number of Candidates Contesting the Election

According to figures released by the Supreme Electoral Commission on 25 October 2011, the total number of candidates running for individual candidacy seats in both houses was 8,627.

Election Monitoring

A Supreme Electoral Commission (SEC) was tasked with supervising and monitoring parliamentary elections from beginning to end.

According to the most recent amendments of the 1956 law on exercise of political rights, SEC is made up of purely judicial members (eleven members). The head of the SEC was Abdel-Moez Ibrahim, chairman of Cairo's Appeal Court.

The 1956 political rights law entrusted the SEC with 16 roles and powers, on top of which are exercising full control of elections, regulating their performance, and ensuring that they are entirely supervised and monitored by judges (a judge for every ballot box).

The SEC was also entrusted with selecting polling and vote-counting stations, preparing voter lists, and regulating and supervising election campaigns in a way that should uphold the ban on raising religious and racial slogans and symbols.

Offenders of SEC's regulations on election campaigns were subject to face prison sentences up to 15 years, and a fine of up to 200,000 EGP.

Election Spending Limits

The SEC placed a 500,000 EGP ceiling on campaign expenditure for independent candidates, and 1 million EGP for party lists.

International Monitoring of the Election

SEC's chairman Abdel-Moez Ibrahim has stated that international monitors and media were welcome to take part in "following"—rather than officially "observing"—the parliamentary election.

Participating Political Parties and Coalitions

- Democratic Alliance for Egypt
- Egyptian Bloc
- Islamist Bloc (Alliance for Egypt)
- Revolution Continues Alliance
- Al-Wafd Party
- Al-Wasat Party
- Al-Adl Party
- Reform and Development Party - Misruna
- NDP Offshoots
- Other Parties

A Voter's Checklist for the Egyptian Elections

What do I need to choose?

As a voter you are expected to choose:
- Two individual candidates to represent you
- One party/coalition list that you feel represents you

Who can I choose from the individual candidates?

You may choose any individual candidates in any combination:
- One professional, one worker/farmer
- Two professionals
- Two workers/farmers

What's in a list?

A list contains a set of candidates listed according to priority. Each list can have candidates from more than one party. The most likely candidate to win out of the list is the one at the top of the list.

What are the lists in the 2011/2012 election?

The lists include:
- The Egyptian Bloc: The Egyptian Bloc includes three parties: the Free Egyptians Party, the Egyptian Social Democratic Party, and the Al-Tagammu Party.
- The Revolution Continues: The Revolution Continues list includes the Socialist Popular Alliance Party, the Egyptian Socialist Party, Egypt Freedom Party, Equality and Development Party, the Egyptian Current Party, and the Revolution's Youth Coalition.
- Al-Nour: This list is also known as the Islamist Bloc, but the entry is under the name of the Al-Nour Party. This list contains candidates from Al-Nour, Al-Asala, and the Building and Development Party.
- Freedom and Justice: This list is also known as the Democratic Alliance for Egypt. It includes the Freedom and Justice Party as its main contributor of candidates along with several other parties, including Ghad Al-Thawra Party, Al-Karama Party, and many others.
- Al-Wafd Party.
- Al-Wasat Party.
- Reform and Development Party.
- Others.

What do you need to do before voting?

- Find out where you are registered by visiting www.elections2011.eg or by calling 140.
- Be prepared with your National ID number.
- Make sure you know where to vote.
- Make sure you do your research about the candidates and lists you are going to choose.

What do you need to do during voting?

You will be given two forms, one for choosing individual candidates in your district's individual-candidacy race, and one for choosing a list in your district's party-list race. Make absolutely sure that you place the form for the individuals in the box designated for individuals and place the form for the list in the box designated for the list. If not, your vote will be invalidated.

How Are Seat Winners Determined in the Egyptian Elections?

Wael Eskandar

The new electoral system in Egypt's 2011/2012 parliamentary races may seem overwhelming from the perspective of those trying to figure out how seat winners are determined. The introduction of the party list system, along with the "largest remainders" seat allocation method, has been a cause for confusion. Also another source of confusion pertains to the individual candidacy system, in which candidates are grouped into three categories—"professional," "worker," or "farmer" (*fellah*)—in order to fulfill the requirement that at least half of parliamentary seats are allocated to workers and farmers.

How Winners are Determined in Individual Candidacy Races per District

Each individual candidacy race district has two seats to be awarded to two candidates. At least one of them must be a worker/farmer.

Winners

In the first round a candidate may win a seat by getting a number of votes greater than 50% of the total number of ballots (50% +1). In other words, if a total of 10,000 voters cast their ballots correctly, a candidate would have to get 5001 votes or more to win a seat in the first round of voting.

Since every voter must choose two candidates, each ballot contains two votes. This means the total number of votes made available by 10,000 voters will be 20,000 votes. It is, therefore, possible for two candidates to each win 5001 votes in the first round. Two candidates winning 5001 votes or more can secure seats in parliament without a runoff, provided one of them is a worker/farmer.

Runoffs and the 50% Worker/Farmer Rule

The following are the different cases for which there is a runoff, either no candidates won, or one of them did:

If no candidate managed to secure 50%+1 of the total valid ballots cast, then the runoff will include the top four candidates provided that at least two of them are worker/farmer candidates, and that at least one of the runoff winners is a worker/farmer candidate.

If the winner in the first round was a professional, the top two worker/farmer candidates compete in a second round.

If the first round winner was a worker/farmer, the next two candidates with the highest votes compete in a second round irrespective of whether they are professional or worker/farmer candidates.

If two professional candidates secured 50%+1 of the valid ballots cast in the first round, then only the one with the highest number of votes will be declared a first round winner, and the top two worker/farmer candidates will compete in a second round.

How List Winners Are Determined Per District

Each district will have several seats to be distributed to the party/coalition lists participating in that district's election. A single district may have four, six, eight, ten, or twelve seats up for grabs.

How are lists ordered?

Party/coalition lists are ordered in such a way so that no two consecutive professionals appear on the list. Any candidate can be placed on the top of the list.

Seat Cost

Each district is assigned a number of party/coalition list seats. Each seat has a theoretical "cost" expressed in terms of votes. The "cost" of a party/coalition list seat in a given district is the total number of valid votes cast, divided by the number of available seats. For example if there were 100,000 votes in a district where 4 seats are up for grabs, the cost of 1 seat would be 25,000 votes. If there were 8 seats, the cost of one seat would be 12,500 votes.

Let us take the example of one seat costing 25,000 votes. If one list receives over 25,000 votes it will be granted one seat. If a list receives over 50,000 votes, it will get 2 seats.

What about fractions of a seat?

Fractions of the full theoretical cost of a seat follow certain rules determined by a seat allocation method called largest remainders. In its simplest form, after all the whole seat quota (e.g. 25,000) has been deducted from the total number of votes received by each party, the highest vote remaining for any of the lists receives a seat.

Example:

Total number of valid votes: 100,000

Number of seats in district: 4

Cost of one seat = Total number of valid votes / Number of seats = 25,000

6 lists, 4 seats in contention

List Name	Votes	Seats Won	Remainder
The Revolution Continues	40,000	1	15,000
Freedom and Justice	23,000	0	23,000
The Egyptian Bloc	12,000	0	12,000
Al-Wasat	17,000	0	17,000
Al-Wafd	5,000	0	5,000
Al-Nour	3,000	0	3,000

Because the Revolution Continues got more than the quota or fulfilled the "cost" for one seat, it is awarded a seat. The rest of the parties did not get enough votes to secure one seat. So where do the remaining three seats go? They go to the largest remainders after the full votes for a complete seat have been subtracted from each party's vote total.

The three highest remainders are: Freedom and Justice Party (23k), Al-Wasat (17k), and Revolution Continues (15k).

The three seats go to the three largest remainders.

Nationwide Threshold

In order for a list to be eligible to win any of party/coalition list seats, it must have won at least 0.5% of the nationwide valid votes.

How Are Seats Allocated Within the List?

Each list has a set of candidates ordered by priority. That order of priority determines which candidates will be selected from a given list to occupy the seats won by that same list, if any. If for example a given list wins three seats, the first three individuals on the list will have seats in parliament.

50% Worker/Farmer Rule

The exception to this rule comes up when "professional" party list candidates who got elected to parliament are more than 50% of the total party list winners. If "professionals" in parliament exceed "workers/farmers" by one, one of the lists will have to skip one of its professional candidates and give the seat to the next worker/ farmer candidate on the list. The list that would have to suffer this is the one with the smallest "coefficient."

A "coefficient" for a given list is calculated as follows = total number of valid ballots / number of seats won by list.

Nationwide Numbers for People's Assembly

Seats

- Number of elected individual-candidacy seats: **166** (1/3 of total seats)
- Number of elected list seats: **332** (2/3 of total seats)
- Total Number of elected seats: **498**
- Percentage of seats that must be held by farmers/workers: **At least 50%**

Electoral Districts/Constituencies

- Total number of electoral districts / constituencies for lists: **46**
- Total number of electoral districts / constituencies for individual candidacy: **83**

Seats per district/constituency for party/coalition lists

- Fifteen districts have four seats
- One district has six seats
- Nineteen districts have eight seats
- Nine districts have ten seats
- Two districts have twelve seats

Laws That Govern Egyptian Elections

Egypt's first parliamentary elections following the January 25 Revolution were governed by three major laws. The People's Assembly Law and the Shura Council Law regulated the selection and performance of the two houses of parliament, whereas the Law on the Exercise of Political Rights regulated the manner in which citizens can vote and run for office.

About the Law on the Exercise of Political Rights

A law regulating the exercise of political rights in Egypt was passed in 1956, ahead of Egypt's first parliamentary elections that followed the 1952 revolution.

The Law on the Exercise of Political Rights (no.73/1956) sets rules for the eligibility of candidates and voters and describes the manner in which the elections are conducted. It has been amended over twenty times since 1956.

On 20 July 2011, the Supreme Council of the Armed Forces (SCAF) amended articles 40, 43, 45, 46, 47, 48, 49, and 50 of this law. Most of the amendments were concerned with detailing appropriate punitive measures for using violence, bribes, or religious slogans in elections.

Article 40 states that those who are on the voter rosters and abstain from voting will be fined up to 500 EGP.

Other articles made multiple voting, voting under pretense identity, and voting without being legally eligible punishable by serving one to five years in prison.

According to Article 50, stealing or damaging ballot boxes, or ruining their content, is punishable with imprisonment. Electoral campaigns that invoke religious slogans or sexual or ethnic slurs are punishable by a minimum of three months in prison and a fine ranging from 6,000 EGP to 12,000 EGP.

Articles 43, 45, 46, 47, and 48 set the penalty for insulting election officials, damaging election facilities, hiding or damaging voter rosters, and registering names of voters through illegal means at one to five years in prison. Those who violate these terms may also be subject to fines from 10,000 EGP to 100,000 EGP.

Using force to prevent anyone from voting or forcing anyone to vote for a certain candidate, as well as spreading rumors about the elections or candidates in a bid to influence the outcome of voting, are also punishable by imprisonment. The offenders may be banned from running for office for five years.

These tough measures were widely supported by the public. Human rights activists have warned that the definition of some of these offenses are too vague and lend themselves to abuse by law enforcers, especially that of spreading rumors.

Leaders of Islamist parties have also criticized the ban on religious slogans. Prior to the vote, the Muslim Brotherhood (MB)-led Democratic Alliance for Egypt had announced that it would campaign under the slogan "We bear good for Egypt." However, it was reported that the Brotherhood continues to use its controversial slogan "Islam is the solution" in its electoral campaign.

In the lead-up to elections, the chairman of the Supreme Electoral Commission (SEC) warned: "Should any candidate violate the amendments of the political rights law in terms of using religious slogans or obtaining money from foreign states or institutions, the individual in question would be tried by the Supreme Administrative Court."

Under Mubarak, the MB was officially banned. However, its candidates were usually permitted to run as independents, as long as they do not identify themselves as MB members.

Salafist Groups and the Islamic Group (Al-Gamaa Al-Islamiyya) maintained that they are entitled to use religious slogans.

Liberal forces oppose the use of religious slogans in election campaigns. "This reflects the ideology of Islamist parties, which are fond of mixing politics with religion," stated Nabil Zaki, spokesman of the left-wing Al-Tagammu Party.

Following the amendments of 20 July 2011, the Egyptian government issued an executive memorandum explaining the implementation mechanisms for the law. According to the thirty-nine-article memorandum, the SEC would have final say in matters related to supervising the parliamentary elections. The SEC will be in full charge of the election process, from "preparing the lists of voters" to "announcing the results."

According to the memorandum, the committees supervising the elections in all of Egypt's twenty-seven governorates are composed of members of the judiciary.

"These committees will make sure that voters have easy access to voting lists ahead of the elections," SEC chief Abdel-Moez Ibrahim said during the lead-up to the vote.

The SEC formed three subcommittees to prepare a database of Egyptian voters. "The first subcommittee will take charge of clearing voter lists of the deceased and emigrants; the second will compile the names of newly eligible voters; and the third will be entrusted with adding the names to the lists," Ibrahim said.

The first subcommittee, headed by Samir Abul Maati, has added the names of individuals stripped from exercising their political rights during the Mubarak era to the lists of voters.

"Voter lists will be made available in both print and electronic form," Abul Maati had promised, adding that complete print lists, indicating the exact number of voters registered at each polling station, would be available at police stations and courts.

"Hundreds of copies will also be made available to citizens to make it easier for them to vote. In addition, the lists will be available on the SEC's official website," he said.

The second subcommittee was tasked with updating voter lists, drawing on data made available by the Civil Status Authority, the Ministry of Interior, the Ministry of Health, and the prosecution authorities. The third subcommittee was responsible for determining the exact number of eligible voters and organizing the polling stations accordingly.

"The judge responsible for each committee will ensure that the polling states operate in a way that allows for the smooth running of a secret ballot," said Abul Maati.

Civil society organizations have welcomed the executive regulations. "It is essential to overhaul voter lists," says Hafez Abu Saeda, chairman of the Egyptian Organization for Human Rights (EOHR).

"The voter lists had been repeatedly exploited by the former regime to rig election results. All we need now is for civil society organizations to have free access and all necessary help in monitoring the poll," Abu Seada added.

About the People's Assembly Law

The People's Assembly, Egypt's lower house of parliament, is governed in accordance with Law 28 for 1972, commonly known as the People's Assembly Law.

This law was first introduced right after late president Anwar Sadat changed the parliament's name from the National Assembly to the People's Assembly and introduced a new constitution in September 1971.

The People's Assembly Law regulates the relationship between parliament and the government, defines the duties and responsibilities of elected deputies, and describes the way in which elections are held. Loyal to a socialist-leaning tradition that was first introduced in the 1952 revolution, the law sets aside half of the assembly's seats for workers and farmers.

In the 1980s, the law was amended to introduce elections through party lists, also known as the proportional representation system. The earlier system of single-seat candidacy was thus abolished.

In 1990, another amendment scrapped the party lists system and reinstituted the old system of individual candidacy.

On 20 September 2011, the Supreme Council of the Armed Forces (SCAF) amended the law yet again, lowering the age of candidacy from thirty to twenty-five years. According to this particular version of the law, fifty percent of the seats would have been elected through the individual candidacy system and fifty percent through party list races, adhering to a proportional representation system.

The raft of amendments also annulled the women's quota system introduced by the Hosni Mubarak regime in 2010. However, the law now stipulates that all party lists must include at least one woman.

To qualify for membership in the assembly, a party list must win at least half a percentage point of nationwide valid votes.

Many political parties criticized the continued reliance on individual candidacy systems, arguing that it gives the powerful supporters of Mubarak's ousted regime a chance to get reelected through vote-buying and bullying.

On 25 September 2011, SCAF amended the People's Assembly Law once more, reducing the number of seats elected through individual candidacy from 50 percent to 33.3 percent.

According to the final version of the law, of the People's Assembly's 508 seats, 332 will be elected through party lists, 166 will be elected through individual candidacy races, and 10 will be appointed by the president. SCAF held presidential powers throughout the course of the 2011/2012 parliamentary elections.

In an earlier draft of the People's Assembly Law, SCAF barred political parties from contesting individual candidacy race seats (i.e. one-third of the available seats in parliament), confining them to party list seats. Under this article, only independent candidates who are not affiliated with a political party would be able to contest individual candidacy race seats. This stipulation, commonly known as Article 5, was rescinded on 8 October 2011 due to strong resistance from various political parties. Ultimately, political parties were able to field candidates in party list races and individual candidacy races.

About the Shura Council Law

The late president Anwar Sadat created the upper house of parliament, known as the Shura Council, in 1980.

Law 120 defines the powers of that council, as well as the manner of selecting its members.

Although the role of the Shura Council is mainly advisory (*shura* means consultation in Arabic), the council is responsible for preparing studies on questions of national concern. The council is also tasked with examining and revising government bills ahead of submission to the People's Assembly, the parliament's lower house.

In the 1980s, this law was amended to allow members of the council to be elected through a system of proportional representation based on party lists, rather than individual candidacy races.

In 1990, the law was amended once more to reinstate the individual candidacy, winner-takes-all electoral system.

On 23 July 2011, the Supreme Council of the Armed Forces (SCAF) amended the Shura Council law yet again, lowering the age requirement for candidates from thirty to twenty-five years.

Of the 270 Shura Council members, 90 were appointed by the president, 60 elected through individual-candidacy races, and 120 elected through party list races.

Each party list must include at least one woman and should win at least half a percentage point of nationwide valid votes.

According to the law, disputes concerning candidacy bids will be referred to the Supreme Administrative Court, while disputes concerning electoral results will be examined by the Higher Court of Appeals (also known as the Court of Cassation).

5 | Looking Forward
Post-Elections Egypt: Revolution or Pact?

Hesham Sallam

[This piece was published in collaboration with Georgetown University's Center for Contemporary Arab Studies (CCAS) as part of Jadaliyya's Egypt Elections Watch. It appeared in the Winter-Spring 2012 CCAS Newsletter.]

For many people, it is compelling, if not intuitive, to think of Egypt's parliamentary elections as a logical extension of what Egyptians started on 25 January 2011. Elections, the conventional reasoning goes, are a critical step in Egypt's transition toward a democratic form of governance that is poised to replace the decades-old rule of former President Hosni Mubarak's now-defunct National Democratic Party. Seen from the inside, however, this reasoning seems fairly detached from a much more complex reality.

The Universe of Transition

It has become embarrassingly obvious for most Egyptians that the advent of parliamentary elections has divided the country into two "universes" that, for the time being, seem very distant from one another: the *universe of transition* and the *universe of revolution*. The *universe of transition* is occupied and led by the Supreme Council of the Armed Forces (SCAF) and a host of elite politicians who, for different reasons, have advanced the narrative that Egypt's revolution and its goals will find a new life in organized politics, including electoral institutions and national legislatures.

The SCAF sees the recent elections as a way to channel unruly political dissent into an organized sector that it can easily manipulate and control through legal engineering and limited pacts. Specifically, the SCAF sees in the elections, the parliament they are yielding, and the constitution that this parliament will produce, an opportunity to work with elite politicians to carve out a political system in which competitive elections and national legislatures would not pose any meaningful threats to the military establishment's longstanding political and economic privileges. Of more immediate concern to the officers, at a time when Mubarak and his associates face trial for murdering peaceful protesters, SCAF members fear that they could face prosecution for similar charges unless they shepherd this transition through an exclusive political process that they can manage and control.

For their part, establishment "politicians" who have secured significant gains at the ballot boxes, chief among them the Muslim Brotherhood's Freedom and Justice Party (FJP), see in the formal political arena an opportunity to secure the upper hand in shaping the rules of the political game, not to mention making critical policy decisions in the near future. While working obediently through the SCAF-designed legal framework puts them in a weak position vis-à-vis the military establishment, it strengthens them vis-à-vis other members of the political community that failed to garner the same electoral agility demonstrated by groups like the FJP, the Salafist Al-Nour Party, and, to a lesser extent, the liberal Al-Wafd Party as well as the secular-leaning coalition known as the Egyptian Bloc. Thus, it was not surprising to hear voices from inside the Muslim Brotherhood suggesting that the group is ready to entertain a pact with SCAF that would give military institutions and their leaders some form of reserved powers in the new constitution such that they would remain beyond the reach of public transparency and parliamentary oversight. Nor was it surprising to hear a tacit silence from other political leaders who seem, at best, ambivalent about this alleged pact.

The Universe of Revolution

Apart from ballot boxes, vote-counts, and parliamentary politics, the *universe of revolution* encompasses all the groups and protest movements that have refused to cede to the SCAF's demand to demobilize and work through—if not, defer to—SCAF-sponsored formal political channels (e.g., elections) in advancing their agendas and objectives. These activists remain convinced that in light of SCAF's demonstrated determination to limit the scope and depth of this transition through legal engineering, repressive practices, and deadly violence, "Egypt's 25 January Revolution" will remain an inconclusive struggle until military leaders step aside and make way for more transformative changes. Whereas the *universe of transition* sees Egypt advancing through an interim transitional framework, the *universe of revolution* sees Egypt suffocating under the rule of military dictatorship.

From the perspective of those who inhabit the *universe of revolution*, the critical battle at hand is not convening free and fair elections, but giving these elections depth and meaning— by ensuring that real power in the remainder of this transition and over future decision-making rests within institutions that are truly accountable, transparent, and responsive to popular demands. For them, achieving the goals of this Revolution—bread, freedom, and social justice—requires much deeper transformations in the Egyptian state than what the SCAF-managed transition can possibly offer. Specifically, the real challenge they see is in the task of taming unruly bureaucracies that shape the daily lives of millions of Egyptian in order to make them more transparent, accountable, and responsive to public needs. These bureaucracies include military institutions—the alleged guardians of this so-called transition—that still dominate significant sectors of the Egyptian economy and state resources, all outside the framework of public transparency and parliamentary oversight. They also include the Ministry of Interior, which continues to host Mubarak's coercive apparatus that has yet to cease its old ways, as evidenced by the deadly violence it has repeatedly employed against unarmed protesters in the past ten months and its persistent intimidation and arrests of political activists. To this list must be added the Ministry of Information, which remains an instrument of propaganda for wielders of power, especially in their current efforts to publicly stigmatize political dissent using tactics not dissimilar to those followed during the Mubarak era. Also included are the Ministry of Finance and other government bodies that make economic decisions affecting the lives of millions of Egyptians away from any form of public deliberation or transparency.

For the committed activists who occupy the *universe of revolution*, overhauling these institutions cannot be achieved through a SCAF-designed political system that accommodates and privileges unaccountable sectors of power inside the Egyptian state. In other words, those who have persistently gathered in public squares in protest of SCAF's rule over the past ten months seek a transformative revolution, not a limited pact with the officers. These activists view the January 25 Revolution as a rebellion against not only the rule of Mubarak, but also against elitist politicians who have a long history of underhanded deals with the former president—deals that, for many, resemble the emerging pact between the military and the winners of the parliamentary elections.

Contesting Interpretations: A Year Later

The tension between the u*niverse of transition* and the *universe of revolution* was perhaps most pronounced during preparations for 25 January 2012, the first anniversary of the eighteen-day uprising that toppled Mubarak. SCAF, as well as major organized political groups like the Muslim Brotherhood, treated this day as one of celebration, with the clear assumption (and perhaps message) that the goals of the revolution have decisively been accomplished through elections. Occupants of the *universe of revolution*, on the other hand, saw no reason to celebrate with the military still in charge, and viewed 25 January 2012 as an opportunity to contest and resist SCAF's domineering role in determining the future of this country. As candidates and parties closely followed vote tallies, activists and protest movements worked tirelessly to spread awareness of both the abuse that Egyptians have suffered at the hands of security forces under SCAF's leadership as well as of the nation-wide protests held on 25 January. While the *universe of transition* wanted to make that day about 25 January 2011, the *universe of revolution* was determined to make it about 25 January 2012, and what will follow it.

Free and fair elections are an integral part of any established democracy. However, for students of politics, whether elections alone can be the vehicle for attaining a truly democratic system remains—at best—debatable. In a context in which Egyptians have to grab onto their gas masks and helmets every time they go out to peacefully express their political views, there is only so much that elections can achieve by themselves. Thus, whether or not the recent elections will be a channel for advancing the type of transformative change that Egyptians called for on 25 January 2011, depends on the ability of popular pressure coming from the *universe of revolution* to trump elitist pacts and to have its say in debates over Egypt's emerging political and social order.

Egypt today faces a choice between an officers-politicians pact that could help the country "transition" to a managed form of limited political competition and participation, versus a much more comprehensive process of revolutionary change dictated and advanced by popular pressures and demands. More specifically, on 25 January 2012, Egyptians faced a choice between celebrating the anniversary of their revolution while deferring to the "elders" to negotiate their future, or taking matters into their own hands and building upon the memory of 25 January to finish what they started one year ago.

6 | Results of the 2011-2012 Parliamentary Elections

This section includes the final results for the 2011/2012 Egyptian parliamentary elections, and a list of the members elected for each district for both the individual candidacy and party list seats.

Final Results of the 2011-2012 Parliamentary Elections

Party/List	Votes	Vote %	Total Seats	PR Seats	IC Seats
Democratic Alliance for Egypt	10,138,134	37.5	235	127	108
Islamist Bloc (led by Al-Nour)	7,534,266	27.8	123	96	27
Al-Wafd	2,480,391	9.2	38	36	2
Egyptian Bloc	2,402,238	8.9	34	33	1
Al-Wasat	989,003	3.7	10	10	0
Revolution Continues	745,863	2.8	7	7	0
Reform and Development	604,415	2.2	9	8	1
Freedom	514,029	1.9	4	4	0
National Party of Egypt	425,021	1.6	5	4	1
Egyptian Citizen	235,395	0.9	4	3	1
Union	141,382	0.5	2	2	0
Conservatives	272,910	1	1	0	1
Democratic Peace	248,281	0.9	1	1	0
Al-Adl	184,553	0.7	1	0	1
Arab Egyptian Unity	149,253	0.6	1	1	0
Independents	-	-	23	-	23

Party/List	Votes	Vote %	Total Seats	PR Seats	IC Seats
Subtotal	27,065,135	100			
SCAF appointees	-	-	10	-	-
Total			508	332	166

Source: *Al-Ahram* (http://www.ahram.org.eg/The-First/News/126247.aspx) and *Al-Masry Al-Youm* (http://www.almasryalyoum.com/node/611851)

LIST OF PEOPLE'S ASSEMBLY MEMBERS ELECTED IN 2011-2012 BY DISTRICT

This section lists the members of parliament elected in the 2011/2012 parliamentary elections by district. The People's Assembly had 508 seats. Of these, 498 of them were to be elected and the remaining 10 appointed by the president, which in this case meant that SCAF appointed them because it was holding presidential powers at the time. Of the 498 elected members, 332 members (two-thirds) were to be elected through party lists, while the remaining 166 members (one-third) were to be elected through individual candidacy races.

Note About Member Types

According to the People's Assembly Law, at least fifty percent of the seats in the People's Assembly are reserved for workers and farmers. Members are therefore classified into several categories, which are listed in the chart below:

F- Farmer (*fellah*)

P- Professional

L - Labor

I. Party List Seats

Cairo

Cairo-1
Hazim Mohamed Farouq Abdel Khaleq (FJP, P)
Rafet Hamed Tawfiq Al-Addawi (FJP, L)
Amin Suleiman Iskandar Suleiman (Al-Karama, P)
Mohamed Abdel Rashid El-Sayed Salama (FJP, L)
Imad Gad Bedres Badrous (Egyptian Social Democratic, P)
Khaled Mohamed Abdel Aziz Chaaban (Al-Tagammu, L)
Bassem Mohamed Kamel Hamed Nasser (Egyptian Social Democratic, P)
Mamdouh Ahmad Ismail Ahmad (Al-Asala, P)
Mahmoud Abdallah Abdel Rassoul (Al-Nour, L)
Tareq Mohamed Sabaq Hussein (Al-Wafd, L)

Cairo-2
Ahmad Imam Ali Abdel Hamid (FJP, L)
Abdel Basset Abdel Hay Mostafa Ismail (FJP, L)
Mohamed Magdy Ali Hamed Qarqar (Labor, P)
Bassel Mohamed Adil Ibrahim (Free Egyptians, P)
Atef Mohamed Bayoumy Makhalif (Free Egyptians, F)
Adel Abdel Maqsod Afifi (Al-Asala, P)
Maged Mohamed Al-Sayed Moussa (Al-Wasat, L)
Margherite Azer (Al-Wafd, L)

Cairo-3
Wahid Mohamed Abdel Magid (Democratic Alliance for Egypt, P)
Adel Abdel Aati Abdel Hamid (FJP, L)
Gamal Hanafi Gamal Ali (FJP, P)
Ahmad Hassan Helmy Said (Free Egyptians, P)
Ayman Taha Khalil Mohamed Mohamed (Free Egyptians, L)
Ashraf Mostafa Hussein Ali (Al-Nour, P)
Ali Ahmad Darwish (Al-Nour, L)
Mohamed Hussein Mohamed Al-Malky (Al-Wafd, L)

Cairo-4
Ossama Yassine Abdel Wahab Mohamed (FJP, P)
Al Mohamady Abdel Maqsod Mohamed (FJP, L)
Hatem Abu Bakr Ahmad Azzam (Civilization, P)

Adel Hamed Mostafa (FJP, L)
Mohamed Ahmed Aata Aamara (Al-Nour, P)
Mahmoud Ghorayeb Abdel Hafez (Al-Nour, L)
Ziad Abdel Hamid Al-Elimy (Egyptian Social Democratic, P)
Mahmoud Ezzelarab Mohamed Al-Saqa (Al-Wafd, P)
Abdel Hakim Ismail Eid (Revolution Continues, L)
Gamal Mostafa Abdel Matloub Kessab (Al-Wasat, L)

Alexandria

Alexandria-1
Sobhy Saleh Moussa Abu Assi (FJP, P)
Salah Naaman Mubarak Bilal (FJP, L)
Ashraf Thabet Saadeddine Al-Sayed (Al-Nour, P)
Mohamed Ramadan Ali Younes (Al-Nour, F)
Hosni Hafez Ibrahim Mohamed (Al-Wafd, L)
Ibrahim Abdel Wahab Mohi Eddine Abu Ahmad (Free Egyptians, P)

Alexandria-2
Hussein Mohamed Ibrahim Hussein (FJP, P)
Ahmad Gad El-Rab Mahmoud Ahmad (FJP, L)
Hassan Prince Hassan Baddar (FJP, P)
Karam Abdel Hamid Al-Sadeq (FJP, L)
Ahmad Khalil Abdel Aziz Kheirallah (Al-Nour, P)
Ahmad Abdel Hamid Abdel Hamid Sayed (Al-Nour, F)
Talaat Marzoq Abdel Aziz Saad (Al-Nour, P)
Abul Ez Hassan Ali Al-Hariri (Revolution Continues, P)
Ali Mohamad Ahmad (Free Egyptians, F)
Hassan Abdel Aziz Ahmad Ali (Al-Wafd, L)
Ali Ezzeddin Thabet Ali (FJP, P)

Assiut

Assiut-1
Mahmoud Helmy Ibrahim Fares (FJP, L)
Mohamed Hamed Ahmad Othman (FJP, P)
Abdel Moneim Hussein Al-Tunsi (FJP, L)
Mahmoud Mohamed Mostafa Abdallah (Al-Nour, P)
Mohamed Ferghali Sherif Ferghali (Egyptian Social Democratic, P)
Helmy Samuel Azer (Egyptian Social Democratic, L)

Ahmad Montasser Mahmoud Salim (Al-Wafd, L)
Mohamed Abdel Aziz Sayed Khalifa (FJP, P)

Assiut-2
Momtaz Ahmad Ali Nasser (FJP, F)
Ferghali Mohamed Ferghali Ahmad (FJP, P)
Mohamed Ahmad Hussein Mahran (Al-Nour, P)
Hamada Imam Ahmad Aatiya (Al-Nour, L)
Ziad Ahmad Bahaeddine (Egyptian Social Democratic, P)
Sana Ahmad Gamaleddine (Egyptian Social Democratic, L)
Ahmad Metwali Mohamed Nasser (Building & Development, L)

Luxor
Abdel Hamid Al-Sanoussi Abdallah (FJP, P)
Bahieddine Mohamed Abdel Dayem Mansour (FJP, L)
Al Hassan Bakri Nubi Ahmad (Al-Nour, P)
Nassreddine Mahmoud Moghazi (Al-Tagammu, L)

Fayoum

Fayoum-1
Ahmed Mohamed Abdel Rahman Abdel Hadi (FJP, P)
Ahmed Ibrahim Bayoumi Sabra (FJP, L)
Sami Salama Naaman (FJP, P)
Nasser Mahmoud Abbas (FJP, L)
Hamada Mohamed Suleiman Awda (Al-Nour, P)
Mostafa Abdel Latif Mahmoud (Al-Nour, F)
Nassreddine Sherif Abdel Ati (Revolution Continues, L)
Yasser Abdel Towab Salloum (Freedom, F)

Fayoum-2
Ahmadi Qassem Mohamed Saad (FJP, L)
Hatem Abdel Azim Abul Hassab Ali (FJP, P)
Oweiss Yassine Ali Awad (Al-Nour, F)
Wagih Abdel Qader Chaaban (Al-Nour, P)

Port Said
Ali Mohamed Mostafa Dorra (FJP, P)
Alaeddine Mahmoud Mahmoud Al-Baha'i (Al-Nour, P)
Rashid Awad Mohamed Hatiba (Al-Wasat, L)

Mohamed Kamaleddine Mohamed Gad (Al-Wafd, L)

Damietta
Saber Abdel Sadeq Mohamed Said (FJP, P)
Mohamed Abdel Hamid Mohamed Al-Hadidi (FJP, L)
Mohamed Shawki Ahmed Mohamed Al Bana (FJP, L)
Tarek Hassan Masaad Al-Dessouki (Al-Nour, P)
Salah Al-Said Al-Said Al-Khowli (Al-Nour, L)
Nasser Mostafa Mohamed Shaker (Al-Nour, P)
Issam Abdel Tahman Mohamed Sultan (Al-Wasat, P)
Hanan Saad Abul Ghayt Hassan (Al-Wafd, L)

Kafr El-Sheikh

Kafr El-Sheikh-1
Hassan Ali Abu Shaaishaa Ali (FJP, P)
Abdallah Ahmad Hamed Ahmad Al-Handawi (FJP, L)
Nasri Saad Ibrahim Al-Daransi (Al-Karama, P)
Al Sayed Mostafa Hussein Khalifa (Al-Nour, P)
Mohamed Fayssal Mohamed Hussein Abidi (Al-Nour, L)
Fawzi Ahmad Abdel Mohsen Hamed (Al-Nour, P)
Mohamed Abdel Hakim Mohamed Hegazi (Al-Wafd, L)
Mohamed Abdel Hamid Mohamed Hashem (Building & Development, L)

Kafr El-Sheikh-2
Ragab Mohamed Mohamed Al-Bana (FJP, P)
Mostafa Mohamed Mostafa Draz (Al-Nour, F)
Yasser Al-Bahey Mohamed Barakat (Al-Wafd, P)
Fathi Abdel Aziz Ibrahim Abdo ((National Party of Egypt, L)

Red Sea
Mohamed Awad Abdel Aal Abdel Hamid (FJP, P)
Zein Al-Abdeen Imbarak Ali (FJP, L)
Sameh Fekry Makram Abid (Free Egyptians, P)
Chaaban Mohamed Ahmad Hussein (Egyptian Citizen L)

Beheira

Beheira-1
Mohamed Gamal Ahmed Heshmat (FJP, P)
Mohamed Awad Al-Zeyat (FJP, L)
Mahdy Abdel Hamid Mohamed Karsham (FJP, L)
Mohamed Abdel Kafi Hamd Mansour (FJP, F)
Younes Zaki Abdel Halim Makhioun (Al-Nour, P)
Abdel Aziz Abdel Rabah Abdel Hamid (Al-Nour, F)
Gamal Abdel Mohsen Ali Qoreitem (Al-Nour, P)
Ibrahim Ragheb Ibrahim Abdo (Al-Nour, L)
Khaled Abdel Mawli Abdel Razeq Khatab (Al-Nour, P)
Wagih Abdel Fadil Issawi (Free Egyptians, F)
Ashraf Mohamed Awad (Al-Wafd, P)
Adel Saad Gad Allah Chaalan (Egyptian Citizen F)

Beheira-2
Mohamed Ibrahim Abdel Matlob Al-Howari (FJP, P)
Mohamed Shaaban Mohamed Issa (FJP, F)
Mohamed Monib Ibrahim Gneidi (Al-Karama, P)
Alaeddine Saad Othman Amer (Al-Nour, P)
Abdel Aziz Sobhy Abdel Aziz Amara (Al-Nour, F)
Mohamed Hafez Mohamed Al-Naamani (Al-Nour, P)
Abdel Fatah Mohamed Abdel Fatah Harhash (Al-Wafd, L)
Mohamed Shawki Khalil Badr (Union, F)

Giza

Giza-1
Issam Eddine Mohamed Al-Aaryan (FJP, P)
Azb Mostafa Morsi Yakot (FJP, L)
Gomaa Mohamed Al-Badri Mari (FJP, P)
Ahmed Abdo Mohamed Sayed (FJP, L)
Mohamed Abdel Wahab Hassan Al-Kurdi (Al-Nour, P)
Abdel Bari Abul Aala Abdel Bari (Al-Nour, F)
Ahmed Mohamed Ahmed Hamoda (Al-Nour, P)
Salem Mohamed Abdel Magid Abu Shanab (Free Egyptians, F)
Abdel Wahab Hassan Khalil (Al-Wafd, P)
Mohi Eddine Abdo Labna (Al-Wasat, L)

Giza-2
Helmy Al-Sayed Abdel Aziz Al-Gazar (FJP, P)
Khaled Mahmoud Hamad Al-Azhary (FJP, L)
Kamal Mohamed Rifaii Abu Iita (Al-Karama, P)
Azza Mohamed Ibrahim Al-Garf (FJP, F)
Adel Youssef Hassan Al-Azazy (Al Nour, P)
Nizar Mahmoud Abdel Hamid Ghorab (Al-Nour, P)
Farid Ali Hussein Ali (Al-Nour, F)
Ayman Ahmad Hussein Abul 'Ela (Egyptian Social Democratic, P)
Abdel Rahman Kamal Abbas (Al-Wafd, L)
Mohamed Adly Issa (Al-Wasat, L)

Ismailia
Hamdi Mohamed Mohamed Ismail (FJP, P)
Alaeddine Khalifa Amr Khalifa (FJP, L)
Gamal Ali Ahmad Hassan (Al-Nour, P)
Magdy Hassan Al-Noweishy (Al-Wafd, L)

Sharqiya

Sharqiya-1
Ahmad El-Sayed Ahmad Shehata (FJP, P)
Mo'men Mohamed Ahmad Zaarour (FJP, L)
Rida Abdallah Mohamed Aatwa (FJP, P)
Adel Redwan Othman Mohamed (FJP, L)
Mohamed Hussein Mohamed Sharaf (Al-Nour, P)
Gamal Mohamed Ibrahim Metwali (Al-Nour, F)
Walid Gouda Afifi (Al-Nour, P)
Atef Mohamed Maghoury (Egyptian Social Democratic, L)
Mohamed Hani Dorry Abdel Ghafar Abaza (Al-Wafd, P)
Badr Bara'a Zakhr Naaman (Al-Wasat, L)

Sharqiya-2
Farid Ismail Abdel Halim Khalil (FJP, P)
Ahmad Ali Ibrahim Ez (FJP, F)
Abbas Mohamed Mohamed Mkhaymar (FJP, P)
Mahmoud Al-Sayed Al-Wahid Abdel Hamid (FJP, L)
Ibrahim Abdel Aal Ibrahim Sayed (Al-Nour, P)
Hisham Abdel Aal Ibrahim Salem (Al-Nour, F)
Talaat Imad Eddine Sadeq Ahmad Soueidy (Al-Wafd, P)
Mostafa Imam Mohamed Eidaros Al-Hout (Al-Wafd, F)

Magdy Sabry Abdel Rahim Aaliwa (Free Egyptians, P)
Seif Mohamed Rashad Salama (Egyptian Arab (Union, F)

Suez
Ahmad Mahmoud Mohamed Ibrahim (FJP, P)
Abdel Khaleq Mohamed Abdel Khaleq Ibrahim (Al-Asala, P)
Abbas Mohamed Abbas Gouda (Al-Nour, L)
Hakim Suleiman Mohamed Hussein (Free Egyptians, L)

Menoufiya

Menoufiya-1
Sabry Mohamed Amr Khadr (FJP, P)
Badr Abdel Aziz Mahmoud El-Fellah (FJP, F)
Mohamed Al-Sayed Ibrahim Idriss (Al-Karama, P)
Salah Abdel Maabod Fayd Al-Sayed (Al-Nour, P)
Atef Sayed Ahmad Yassine Kanso (Al-Nour, F)
Issam Mohamed Abdel Hamid Al-Sabahi (Al-Wafd, F)
Ahmed Al-Sayed Al-Sayed Abdel Aal (National Party of Egypt, L)
Ahmad Refaat Mohamed Said (Building & Development, F)

Menoufiya-2
Ashraf Mahmoud Mohamed Badreddine (FJP, P)
Abdel Fatah Mahmoud Eid (FJP, L)
Aatiya Aadlan Aatiya Ramadan (FJP, P)
Mohamed Kamel Mostafa Kamel (Al-Wafd, P)
Mahmoud Abul Seoud Morsi Rish (Al-Wafd, F)
Gamal Mansour Mohamed Abdel Nabi (Al-Nour, P)
Shafiq Mohamed Mohamed Chahine (National Party of Egypt F)
Helmy El-Sayed Ibrahim Mrad (Building & Development, L)

Beni Suef

Beni Suef-1
Hamdy Hussein Mohamed Zahran (FJP, P)
Abdel Rahman Mohamed Shukry Abdel Rahman (FJP, F)
Mahmoud Saber Abdel Gawab Allam (FJP, P)
Shaaban Ahmad Abdel Alim (Al-Nour, P)
Mohamed Mostafa Abdel Hafez (Al-Nour, F)
Mohamed Mahrous Ahmed (Al-Nour, L)

Khaled Hafani Abdallah Ali (Revolution Continues, L)

Beni Suef-2
Saad Abboud Abdel Wahed Katab (Al-Karama, P)
Farouk Abdel Hafiz Abdel Aati Mabrouk (FJP, L)
Mohamed Qorni Abdel Wahab (Egyptian Social Democratic, L)
Abdel Towab Mohamed Mohamed Othman (Al-Nour, P)

Gharbiya

Gharbiya-1
Sayed Ahmad Youssef Al-Sayed Al-Shawry (FJP, L)
Mohamed Mandwa Mohamed Al-Azbawy (FJP, P)
Hamdy Abdel Wahab Ahmad Redwan (FJP, L)
Hany Adel Ahmad Saqr (Al-Nour, P)
Mefreh Mohamed Al-Chazly (Al-Nour, F)
Al Sayed Al-Mohamadi Al-Aagwani (Al-Nour, P)
Mostafa Abdel Raouf Al-Noweihy (Al-Wafd, P)
Hussein Mahmoud Khalil (Al-Wafd, F)
Hamada Ahmed Ibrahim Al-Qost (Free Egyptians, P)
Ashraf Talaat Mohamed Al-Shebrawy (Building & Development, F)

Gharbiya-2
Saad Asmat Mohamed Al-Husseini (FJP, P)
Mohamed Mostafa El-Adly Abdel Wahed (FJP, L)
Alaaeddine Mohamed Ahmad Al-Ezb Al-Qat (FJP, P)
Nagah Saad Mahros Thabet (FJP, L)
Abdel Wahab Mohamed Zaki Farah Al-Badri (Al-Nour, P)
Ahmed Ahmed Abdel Moty Al-Bili (Al-Nour, F)
Ahmed Zaki Ahmed El-Kattan (Al-Nour, P)
Ahmed Mahmoud Ahmed Attallah (Al-Wafd, P)
Nabil Tawfiq Al-Sayed Mtawea (Al-Wafd, F)
Atef Abdel Hay Abdel Rahman Shakhba (Free Egyptians, F)

Qalyubia

Qalyubia-1
Mohamed Imad Eddine Abdel Hamid Saber (FJP, P)
Mohamed Abdel Magid Ibrahim Dessouki (FJP, F)
Nader Abdel Khaleq Abdel Hamid Afifi (Al-Nour, P)

Al Sayed Fouad Ahmad Koush (Al-Wafd, L)

Qalyubia-2
Mohamed Mohamed Ibrahim Al-Beltagy (FJP, P)
Abdallah Ahmad Mohamed Khalil (FJP, L)
Hady Mohamed Anwar Abdelrahman Ghaniyieh (FJP, P)
Hassan El-Sayed Mohamed Abul Azzam Al-Sayed (Al-Nour, P)
Mohamed Hassan Abdel Sallam Hassan (Al-Nour, L)
Mahmoud Abdel Mardi (Al-Nour, P)
Mostafa Ahmad Khalil (Al-Wafd, L)
Fathi Dessouki Sayed Ali (Egyptian Social Democratic, L)

Minya

Minya-1
Mohamed Saad Tawfiq Al-Katatny (FJP, P)
Mohamed Abdel Azim Mohamed Ahmed (FJP, L)
Mohamed Hassan Aref Metwali (FJP, P)
Mostafa Abdel Khaleq Mahdi Al-Sayed (FJP, L)
Amro Magdy Makram Abdel Latif (Building & Development, P)
Saleh Abdel Azim Abdel Fatah (Al-Nour, L)
Ihab Adel Ramzi Hanna (Freedom, P)
Mostafa Morsi Othman Seif Al-Nasser (Al-Wasat, F)

Minya-2
Hussein Sultan Mohamed Nassar (FJP, P)
Bahaeddine Sayed Aatiya Suleiman (FJP, L)
Mohamed Abu Bakr Mohamed Hassan (FJP, P)
Mohamed Khalifa Hussein Amr (Egyptian Social Democratic, P)
Ashraf Sayed Mohamed Shawky (Egyptian Social Democratic, F)
Mohamed Ahmad Mahmoudein Al-Manshad (Al-Nour, F)
Mohamed Talaat Mohamed Othman (Al-Nour, P)
Mohamed Abdel Hafiz Mohamed Abdel Hafiz (Al-Wafd, F)

Qena

Qena-1
Mahmoud Youssef Mahmoud Abdel Rahim (FJP, P)
Mohamed Ahmad Aatiya (FJP, L)
Motaz Mohamed Mahmoud Ali Hassan (Freedom, P)

Hassan Bakri Ahmad Bakri (Al-Nour, F)

Qena-2
Abdel Nasser Teghian Abdel Aal Mahmoud (FJP, P)
Younes Saber Hassan Ali (FJP, L)
Abdel Karim Mohamed Ahmad Ibrahim (Al-Nour, P)
Mohamed Gab Allah Abdel Aziz Mohamed (Al-Nour, F)
Hussein Fayez Abu Aloufa Al-Chazly (Union, P)
Abdel Nabi Mohamed Abdel Nabi Al-Seman (Freedom, F)
Ahmed Mokhtar Othman Mohamed (Al-Wafd, L)
Ibrahim Abdel Mardi (FJP, P)

New Valley
Sameh Sedawi Mohamed Ali (FJP, P)
Salah Abdel Hafez Mohamed Adam (Al-Nour, P)
Kamal Mohamed Mahmoud Abdel Gawad (Al-Nour, L)
Khaled Ismail (Egyptian Bloc L)

Marsa Matruh
Farag Ali El-Abd Abdel Hamid Abdel Mawli (Al-Nour, P)
Khairallah Abdel Aziz Hussein Mardi (Al-Nour, F)
Saad Gab Allah Abu Seif Massoud (Al-Nour, P)
Bilal Gabriel Abdallah (FJP, L)

North Sinai
Suleiman Salem Saleh Salem (FJP, P)
Khaled Mohamed Meslim Ali Selmy (FJP, L)
Mohsen Abdel Aziz Hussein (Al-Nour, P)
Salama Salem Salman Salem (Building & Development, L)
Abdallah Ibrahim El-Dessouki Abdraboh (FJP, P)
Ahmad Ibrahim Kassem Metwali (FJP, L)
Fodiyah Salem Abid Allah Salem (Building & Development, P)
Ahmed Ramadan Abdel Faghour Wahdan (Al-Wafd, L)

Sohag

Sohag-1
Mohamed El-Saghir Abdel Rahim (Building & Development, P)
Ali Bahaeddine Al-Ansari (Al-Nour, L)
Abdel Nasser Hassan Mohamed (Al-Nour, L)

Rafaat Mohamed Suleiman (Al-Nour, F)
Mohamed Aatiyah El-Saghir Hussein (FJP, P)
Mohamed Youssef Mahmoud Shehata (FJP, L)
Mokhtar Ahmed Mohamed Ahmed Al-Sayed (FJP, P)
Hussein Abdel Rahman Ibrahim Abu Douma (Egyptian Social Democratic, F)
Salah Eddine Mohamed Hassan Al-Aagagi (Egyptian Social Democratic, F)
Ahmad Hereidy Mahmoud (Al-Wafd, F)
Mohamed Hamd Sabbaq (Al-Wasat, P)
Ahmad Ahmad Abdallah (Al-Nour, P)

Sohag-2
Mohamed Mostafa Abdel Magid Al-Ansari (FJP, P)
Ali El-Shazli Baddawi Al-Sayed (FJP, P)
Mahmoud Hamdy Ahmad (Al-Nour, P)
Ashraf Ahmad Agour Hassan (Al-Nour, F)
Mohamed Abdel Rahman Halali (Free Egyptians, P)
Abdel Fatah Ali Kassem (Egyptian Citizen F)
Abdel Hakim Hassani (Building & Development, P)
Ahmed Mohamed Ismail (Al-Wasat, F)

Daqahliyya

Daqahliyya-1
Tarek El-Dessouki Abdel Galil Ali (FJP, P)
Siham Abdel Latif Mohamed Al-Imani Al-Gamal (FJP, F)
Adel Younes Mohamed Rashed (FJP, P)
Ibrahim Mohamed Ahmad Abdel Rahman (Al-Nour, P)
Hussein Abdel Gawad Abdel Moty (Al-Nour, F)
Abdel Hamid Mohamed Ibrahim Al-Imam (Al-Wafd, L)
Mohamed Shabana Mohamed Talba (Revolution Continues, P)
Mohamed Ahmad Mohamed Gaber (National Party of Egypt F)

Daqahliyya-2
Mohamed Mohamed Abdel Ghani Farag (FJP, P)
Al Sadat Abdel Rahim Abdel Salam (FJP, L)
Adel Abbas Mohamed Al-Qalla (FJP, P)
Rizk Mohamed Mohamed Ali Ahmed (Al-Nour, F)
Mohamcd Mohamed Hassan Issa (Al-Nour, P)
Mohamed Hamdi Abul Ghayt Mostager El-Gamal (Al-Nour, F)
Ibrahim Mohamed Mohamed Aamasha (Al-Wafd, P)
Magdy Mohamed Ali Al-Khoreibi (Revolution Continues, L)

Daqahliyya-3
Mohamed Abdel Aal Abbas Haykal (FJP, P)
Shafiq Mohamed Abdel Hay Ibrahim Al-Deeb (FJP, L)
Mohamed Ragab Ismail Awaf (FJP, P)
Mostafa Al-Said El-Sawi Mtaweh (Al-Nour, P)
Sherif Taha Hussein Abdel Fadil (Al Nour, F)
Mostafa Abdel Aziz Ahmed Al-Gendi (Revolution Continues, P)
Baddawi Abdel Latif Hilal Baddawi (Al-Wafd, F)
Al Sayed Shehata Mohamed Khalifa (Democratic, Peace L)

Aswan
Shehat Abdallah Amr Ahmed (FJP, F)
Mohamed Mahmoud Hussnein Saleh (Al-Nour, F)
Mohamed Al-Mirghani Abdallah Daoud (Al-Wafd, P)
Hilal Ahmed Al-Dindrawi Mohamed (Al-Tagammu, F)

II. Individual Candidacy Seats

Cairo
Fahmi Abdo Mostafa (FJP, P)
Kamal Hassan Mahdi (FJP, L)
Amro Mohamed Zaki (FJP, P)
Yasser Ibrahim Abdallah (FJP, L)
Mostafa Ahmed Al-Naggar (Al-Adl, P)
Amro Farouk Awda (Independent, L)
Amro Nabil Ahmed Hamzawi (Independent, P)
Hisham Suleiman Moussa (Independent, L)
Sayed Hussein Mohamed Gad Allah (FJP, P)
Ashraf Saad Abdel Latif (FJP, L)
Mohamed Abu Hamed Chedid (Free Egyptians, P)
Mostafa Ferghali Rashwan (FJP, L)
Khaled Mohamed Ahmed Mohamed (FJP, P)
Nassreddine Ibrahim Othman (FJP, L)
Khaled Hanafi Fahim Hussein (FJP, P)
Youssry Mohamed Bayoumi (FJP, L)
Mohamed Mostafa Bakry Mohamed (Independent, P)
Ramadan Ahmed Amr Salem (FJP, L)

Alexandria
Hosny Mohamed Taha Doueidar (Independent, P)
Mostafa Mohamed Mostafa (FJP, L)
Mahmoud Rida Abdel Aziz Al-Khodeiri (Independent, P)
Al Mouhamadi Al-Sayed Ahmed Abul Ahmed (FJP, L)
Mahmoud Aatiya Mabrouk (FJP, P)
Saber Aboul Foutouh Baddawi Al-Sayed (FJP, L)
Issam Mohamed Hussnein (Al-Nour, P)
Issam Mahmoud Ragab (Independent, L)

Kafr El-Sheikh
Mohamed Ibrahim Abdel Hamid Mansour (Al-Nour, P)
Mohamed Abdel Magid Abu Shaaishaa (Al-Nour, F)
Mohamed Ibrahim Darwish Amer (FJP, P)
Ashraf Mohamed Al-Said Youssef (FJP, L)
Youssef El-Badri Abdel Fatah National Party of Egypt P)
Mohamed Abdel Aalim Daoud (Al-Wafd, L)

Damietta
Ali Hassan Hassan Al-Day (FJP, P)
Mohamed El-Sayed Ahmad Abu Moussa (FJP, L)
Mohamed Mohamed Al-Falahi (FJP, P)
Omran Mohamed Mgahed (Independent, L)

Port Said
Akram Al-Mandwa Awad Al-Shaaer (FJP, P)
Al Badri Ferghali Ali (Independent, L)

Fayoum
Adel Ismail Abdel Hamid Moussa (FJP, P)
Hamdi Taha Abdel Rahim El-Issa (FJP, F)
Ossama Yehia Abdel Wahed Yehia (FJP, P)
Sayed Abdel Karim Gaber Nasr (FJP, F)
Gamal Hassan Abdel Latif (FJP, P)
Fawzi Ali Abdel Aziz (FJP, F)

Assiut
Samir Othman Ibrahim Khashba (FJP, P)
Bayoumi Ismail Abdel Gaber (Building & Development, L)
Mohamed Salama Bakr (FJP, P)
Mohamed Modr Moussa (FJP, L)
Abdel Aziz Khalaf Mohamed Ali (FJP, P)
Abdallah Sadeq Nashi Ahmad (FJP, L)
Hassan Ali Abdel Aal Amer (FJP, P)
Amr Abdel Rahim Mahmoud Ali (Building & Development, F)

Luxor
Abdel Mawgoud Rageh Dardiri (FJP, P)
Khaled Abdel Moneim Farrag (Freedom, F)

Red Sea
Mohamed Mahmoud Youssef Katamsh (FJP, P)
Abdel Basset Sayed Moubarak (Egyptian Citizen L)

Beheira
Osama Mohamed Ibrahim Suleiman (FJP, P)
Tarek Ragab Saleh Mohamed Saleh (FJP, L)
Mahmoud Abdallah Ibrahim Mabrouk Heba (Al-Nour, P)

Yasser Ali Abdel Rafea Ali (FJP, F)
Ahmed Zahir Mohamed Said (FJP, P)
Masry Saad Masry Mohareb (FJP, F)
Abdallah Mohamed Mohamed Saad (Al-Nour, P)
Hamed Abdallah Khalil Al-Tahan (Al-Nour, F)
Saad Mahmoud Mohamed Abu Taleb (FJP, P)
Ahmad El-Sayed Youssef Khatar (Independent, L)

Sharqiya
Al Sayed Abdel Aziz Ismail Nagida (FJP, P)
Saleh Ali Ahmed Suleiman (FJP, L)
Amir Mohamed Bassem Al-Naggar (FJP, P)
Mohamed Mohamed Abdel Ra'ouf Ismail (FJP, L)
Mohamed Fayad Abdel Moneim Fayad (FJP, P)
Ibrahim Mohamed Mohamed Salim (FJP, F)
Mohamed Safwat Al-Hadi Sweilem (FJP, P)
Mohamed Awad Mohamed Shawish (FJP, L)
Ahmed Suleiman Ahmed Ibrahim (FJP, P)
Al Sayed Mohamed Abdel Karim Al-Aatwil (FJP, L)
Helmy Al-Sayed Mohamed Bakr (Independent, P)
Saad Mohamed Youssef Hussein (FJP, L)
Mohamed Anwar Aasmat Al-Sadat (Reform & Development F)
Said Al-Azab Abdel Kader Eid (FJP, L)
Nasr Ali Ahmed Tahoun (Independent, P)
Mahmoud Ali Mohamed Abul Magd (FJP, L)
Ibrahim Ibrahim Mostafa Hegag (FJP, P)
Anwar Said Anwar Al-Belkimy (Al-Nour, L)

Giza
Mohamed Ibrahim Ahmed Hussein (FJP, P)
Khatab Sayed Khatab Mourad (FJP, L)
Gamal Abdel Fatah Ali Ashri (FJP, P)
Hassan Breik Khalifa Breik (FJP, L)
Mohamed Amro Mahmoud Al-Shobky (Independent, P)
Ayman Mahmoud Sadeq Refaat (FJP, L)
Mohamed Abdel Moneim Mahmoud Al-Saqy (Civilization, P)
Abdel Salam Zaki Mohamed Bashandi (FJP, L)
Mahmoud Mohamed Ali Amer (FJP, P)
Mostafa Mohamed Ibrahim Salman (Independent, F)

Beni Suef
Gaber Mansour Abdel Wahab Yassine (FJP, P)
Negm Eddine Aziz Fadel Salim (Al-Nour, L)
Mohamed Shaker Abdel Baki Mayhoub (FJP, P)
Abdel Hakim Mohamed Mohamed Massoud (Al-Nour, F)
Nohad Al-Kassem Sayed Abdel Wahab Khadir (FJP, P)
Abdel Kader Abdel Wahab Abdel Kader Ismail (FJP, L)

Sohag
Walid Abdel Awal Mahmoud Ibrahim (Al-Nour, P)
Moustafa Abdel Hamid Ali Abdel Rahim (FJP, F)
Mohamed Mohamed Abdel Rahman Al-Sayed (FJP, P)
Adlan Mahmoud Ahmed Morsy (Building & Development, F)
Mohamed Massoud Al-Imam Al-Harzagi (FJP, P)
Lahzy Ahmed Nagdy Hassan (Building & Development, F)
Gaber Abdel Moneim Ali Mohamed (Building & Development, P)
Fayssal Mohamed Ali Hassan (Independent, F)
Raft Mohamed Mahmoud Ahmed (Independent, P)
Youssef Hassan Youssef Ahmed (Independent, F)

Ismailia
Mohamed Hisham Mostafa Al-Sawly (FJP, P)
Mohamed Abdallah Ali Howary (Al-Nour, F)

Suez
Abbas Abdel Aziz Abbas Mohamed (FJP, P)
Hany Noureddine Abu Bakr (Building & Development, L)

Aswan
Mohamed Mahmoud Ali Hamed (Independent, P)
Farag Allah Gad Allah Ahmed Mahmoud (Building & Development, L)
Mohamed Abdel Hamid Ahmed Al-Faqi (Al-Wafd, P)
Sayed Abdel Maqsoud Askar (FJP, L)
Ali Abdel Fatah Ali Negm (Al-Nour, P)
Mahmoud Ismail Mohdiya (Building & Development, F)
Hamdy El-Dessouki Mohamed Al-Fakhrany (Independent, P)
Mahmoud Tawfiq Mohamed Abdel Aal (FJP, L)
Sameh Abdel Hamid Shawky Ibrahim (FJP, P)
Abel Aziz Yehia Abdel Aziz (FJP, L)
Ibrahim Zakariya Ibrahim Younes (FJP, P)
Maher Mohamed Sayed Shehata (Independent, F)

Daqahliyya
Yousry Mohamed Hany (FJP, P)
Tarek Mohamed Kattab (FJP, L)
Ali Ibrahim Ali Qatamsh (Al-Nour, P)
Saad Ali Abdo Helwagi (FJP, L)
Imad Shamseddine Mohamed Abdel Rahman (FJP, P)
Abdel Hamid Mohamed Hassan Issa (FJP, L)
Ibrahim Ibrahim Abu Awaf Youssef (FJP, P)
Khaled Moustafa Kamel (Independent, L)
Khaled Mohamed Metwali Al-Deeb (FJP, P)
Taher Ahmed El-Said Aata (Independent, F)
Al Sayed Mohamed Niazy Al-Adawi (FJP, P)
Ossama Mohamed Abdel Aata Metwali (Independent, F)

Qalyubia
Mohsen Radi (FJP, P)
Ali Wanes (Al-Nour, L)
Nasser Al-Hafi (FJP, P)
Gamal Shehata (FJP, L)
Ahmed Mohamed Mahmoud Diab (FJP, P)
Sayed Imam Mahmoud Al-Qady (FJP, P)

Minya
Ali Ahmed Mohamed Amran (FJP, P)
Gomaa Youssef Ahmed Kafafi (FJP, L)
Mohamed Abdallah Hassan Al-Bassel (FJP, P)
Hamdy Khalifa Mohamed Abdel Nabi (FJP, L)
Mosharaf Ahmed Mohamed Mosharaf (Al-Nour, P)
Ahmed Hassan Sayed Abboud (Al-Nour, L)
Midhat Abdel Gaber Ali Youssef (Al-Nour, P)
Ahmed Youssef Toni Abul Kheir (Building & Development, F)

Qena
Ahmed Sayed Mohamed Al-Saghir (FJP, P)
Adel Mohamed Abid Ahmed (Building & Development, F)
Mohamed Younes Mohamed Ali (Independent, P)
Hisham Ahmed Hanafi Abdallah (FJP, F)
Ali Ibrahim Mohamed Al-Shayshni (FJP, P)
Abdel Nasser El-Sayed Mohamed Abdel Halim (Building & Development, L)

Marsa Matruh
Mansour Deif (Al-Nour, P)
Mansour Al-Aqari Al-Qoweya (Al-Nour, F)

New Valley
Mohamed Abdel Magid Hamd (FJP, P)
AlaEddine Abdel Latif Ismail (Al-Nour, L)

North Sinai
Abdel Rahman Said Abdel Rahman Daoud (FJP, P)
Ali Mohamed Salman (Independent, L)

South Sinai
Mohamed Farrag Salem Moussa (Al-Nour, P)
Ghorayeb Ahmed Hassan Ali (Independent, L)

ABOUT TADWEEN PUBLISHING

Tadween Publishing is a publishing house seeking to institutionalize a new form of knowledge production. A subsidiary of the Arab Studies Institute, we aim to publish critical texts and to interrogate the existing processes and frameworks through which knowledge is produced. We publish in Arabic, English, and French and there are no restrictions on region or topic.

Arab Studies Institute (ASI) is a not-for-profit organization that produces knowledge on matters related to the Arab world and its relations. An institute in its own right, it also serves as an umbrella organization for five other subsidiaries: the *Arab Studies Journal*, *Jadaliyya*, Quilting Point, FAMA (Forum on Arab and Muslim Affairs), and Tadween Publishing.

Arab Studies Journal is a peer-reviewed, multidisciplinary research publication in the field of Arab and Middle East Studies. *Arab Studies Journal* also publishes occasional themed issues and cutting-edge scholarship on topics that receive short shrift elsewhere. It has an independent editorial board and entered its twentieth year in 2012.

Jadaliyya is an independent e-zine that provides a unique source of insight and critical analysis combining local knowledge, scholarship, and advocacy with an eye to audiences in the United States, the Arab world, and beyond. The site currently publishes posts both in Arabic and in English.

Quilting Point is a production company/organization that operates as a collective, producing research-based documentaries that combine scholarship and audio-visual production. Quilting Point's production team also films and edits conferences and promotional videos for academic institutions.

F.A.M.A. (Forum on Arab and Muslim Affairs) is ASI's research arm. It produces and oversees ASI's research projects on overarching issues related to the Arab and broader Muslim worlds, including the Middle East and North Africa. The forum is the home of ASI's Knowledge Production Project.